Working Papers

Chapters 1-17

Accounting, 26e and Financial Accounting, 14e

Carl S. Warren

Professor Emeritus of Accounting
University of Georgia, Athens

James M. Reeve

Professor Emeritus of Accounting
University of Tennessee, Knoxville

Jonathan E. Duchac

Professor of Accounting
Wake Forest University

CENGAGE Learning

Australia • Brazil • Japan • Korea • Mexico • Singapore • Spain • United Kingdom • United States

CENGAGE Learning

ISBN-13: 978-1-305-39237-3

Cengage Learning
20 Channel Center Street
Boston, MA 02210
USA

Cengage Learning is a leading provider of customized learning solutions with office locations around the globe, including Singapore, the United Kingdom, Australia, Mexico, Brazil, and Japan. Locate your local office at: **www.cengage.com/global**.

Cengage Learning products are represented in Canada by Nelson Education, Ltd.

To learn more about Cengage Learning Solutions, visit **www.cengage.com**.

Purchase any of our products at your local college store or at our preferred online store **www.CengageBrain.com**.

Printed in the United States of America
Print Number: 01 Print Year: 2014

CONTENTS

PREFACE

The working papers include problem-specific forms for preparing solutions for Exercises, A&B Problems, the Continuing Problem, and the Comprehensive Problems from the textbook. These forms, with preprinted headings, provide a structure for the problems, which will help you get started and save you time.

Based on students' testimonials and instructors' feedback, the forms in the working papers have been streamlined to make them simpler to use and to better reflect the changing environment of business. For example, the vertical rules that separated digits of numbers entered into journals, ledgers, and statements have been removed, making it easier to write in numbers.

Note that when entering whole amounts into the forms, your instructor will direct you on whether to include a decimal point and zeroes (e.g., 100.00) or to omit those (e.g., 100).

EXERCISE 1-1

a. 1. ______ 6. ______ 11. ______
2. ______ 7. ______ 12. ______
3. ______ 8. ______ 13. ______
4. ______ 9. ______ 14. ______
5. ______ 10. ______ 15. ______

b. ______

EXERCISE 1-2

______

EXERCISE 1-3

a. 1. ______ 6. ______
2. ______ 7. ______
3. ______ 8. ______
4. ______ 9. ______
5. ______ 10. ______

b. ______

EXERCISE 1-4

______

EXERCISE 1-5

______

EXERCISE 1-6

	Assets	=	Liabilities	+	Owner's Equity
a.	________	=	$376,000	+	$895,000
b.	$1,375,000	=	________	+	$855,000
c.	$863,500	=	$211,000	+	________

EXERCISE 1-7

a. ______________________________

b. ______________________________

c. ______________________________

d. ______________________________

e. ______________________________

EXERCISE 1-8

a. ______________________________

b. ______________________________

c. ______________________________

d. ______________________________

e. ______________________________

f. ______________________________

EXERCISE 1-9

a. ______________________________

b. ______________________________

c. ______________________________

d. ______________________________

e. ______________________________

EXERCISE 1-10

a. (1) Assets: ______________________________

(2) Liabilities: ______________________________

(3) Owner's equity: ______________________________

b. (1) Assets: ______________________________

(2) Liabilities: ______________________________

(3) Owner's equity: ______________________________

EXERCISE 1-10, Concluded

c. ______________________

____

____

____

EXERCISE 1-11

1. Expenses: ______________________
2. Owner's investments: ______________________
3. Owner's withdrawals: ______________________
4. Revenues: ______________________

EXERCISE 1-12

1. ______________________
2. ______________________
3. ______________________
4. ______________________
5. ______________________
6. ______________________
7. ______________________
8. ______________________
9. ______________________
10. ______________________

EXERCISE 1-13

a. (1) ______________________

(2) ______________________

(3) ______________________

(4) ______________________

(5) ______________________

(6) ______________________

(7) ______________________

b. ______________________

c. ______________________

d. ______________________

e. ______________________

EXERCISE 1-14

____

____

____

____

EXERCISE 1-15

Jupiter:		
Mars:		
Saturn:		
Venus:		

EXERCISE 1-16

1. Accounts Receivable: ______________________________
2. Cash: ______________________________
3. Fees Earned: ______________________________
4. Land: ______________________________
5. Mary Bayern, Capital: ______________________________
6. Supplies: ______________________________
7. Supplies Expense: ______________________________
8. Utilities Expense: ______________________________
9. Wages Expense: ______________________________
10. Wages Payable: ______________________________

EXERCISE 1-17

1. Accounts Receivable: ______________________________
2. Cash: ______________________________
3. Fees Earned: ______________________________
4. Land: ______________________________
5. Mary Bayern, Capital: ______________________________
6. Supplies: ______________________________
7. Supplies Expense: ______________________________
8. Utilities Expense: ______________________________
9. Wages Expense: ______________________________
10. Wages Payable: ______________________________

EXERCISE 1-18

a.

Statement of Owner's Equity

EXERCISE 1-18, Concluded

b. ______________________

EXERCISE 1-19

Income Statement

EXERCISE 1-20

Freeman:

Heyward:

Jones:

Ramirez:

EXERCISE 1-21

a.

Balance Sheet

Balance Sheet

b.	
c.	

Name ______________________________

EXERCISE 1-22

a. 1. Accounts payable: ______________________________
2. Cash equivalents: ______________________________
3. Crude oil inventory: ______________________________
4. Equipment: ______________________________
5. Exploration expenses: ______________________________
6. Income taxes payable: ______________________________
7. Investments: ______________________________
8. Long-term debt: ______________________________
9. Marketable securities: ______________________________
10. Notes and loans payable: ______________________________
11. Notes receivable: ______________________________
12. Operating expenses: ______________________________
13. Prepaid taxes: ______________________________
14. Sales: ______________________________
15. Selling expenses: ______________________________

b. ______________________________

____

____

____

c. ______________________________

____

____

EXERCISE 1-23

1. Cash received from fees earned: ______________________________
2. Cash paid for expenses: ______________________________
3. Cash paid for land: ______________________________
4. Cash paid to owner for personal use: ______________________________

EXERCISE 1-24

Statement of Cash Flows

Name ______________________

EXERCISE 1-25

EXERCISE 1-25, Continued

(Optional)

Income Statement

Statement of Owner's Equity

EXERCISE 1-25, Concluded

(Optional)

Balance Sheet

EXERCISE 1-26

a. ______________________________

b. ______________________________

c. ______________________________

EXERCISE 1-27

a. ______________________________

b. ______________________________

c. ______________________________

d. ______________________________

Name ______________________

PROBLEM 1-1 ___

1.

	ASSETS			=	LIABILITIES	+	OWNER'S EQUITY							
	Cash	+ Accounts Receivable	+ Supplies	=	Accounts Payable	+	______, Capital	– ______, Drawing	+ Fees Earned	– Rent Exp.	– Sal. Exp.	– Supp. Exp.	– Auto Exp.	– Misc. Exp.
a.														
b.														
Bal.														
c.														
Bal.														
d.														
Bal.														
e.														
Bal.														
f.														
Bal.														
g.														
Bal.														
h.														
Bal.														
i.														
Bal.														
j.														
Bal.														

PROBLEM 1-1 ___, Concluded

2. ____

____

____

____

3. ____

____

4. ____

____

____

____

PROBLEM 1-2 ___

1.

Income Statement

2.

Statement of Owner's Equity

PROBLEM 1-2 ___, Concluded

3.

Balance Sheet

4. ____

____

PROBLEM 1-3 ___

1.

Income Statement

2.

Statement of Owner's Equity

PROBLEM 1-3 ___, Concluded

3.

Balance Sheet

4. (Optional)

Statement of Cash Flows

PROBLEM 1-4 ___

1.

	ASSETS		=	LIABILITIES	+	OWNER'S EQUITY															
	Cash	+	Supplies	=	Accounts Payable	+	________, Capital	–	________, Drawing	+	Sales Comm.	–	Rent Exp.	–	Sal. Exp.	–	Auto Exp.	–	Supp. Exp.	–	Misc. Exp.
a.																					
b.																					
Bal.																					
c.																					
Bal.																					
d.																					
Bal.																					
e.																					
Bal.																					
f.																					
Bal.																					
g.																					
Bal.																					
h.																					
Bal.																					
i.																					
Bal.																					

PROBLEM 1-4 ___, Continued

2.

Income Statement

Statement of Owner's Equity

PROBLEM 1-4 ___, Concluded

Balance Sheet

This Page Not Used.

Name ______________________________ *Chapter 1*

PROBLEM 1-5 ___

1.

Assets							=	Liabilities	+	Owner's Equity
Cash	+	Accounts Receivable	+	Supplies	+	Land	=	Accounts Payable	+	____________, Capital
________	+	________	+	________	+	________	=	________	+	________, Capital
________________________							=	________	+	________, Capital
________________________							=	________, Capital		

Name ____________________

PROBLEM 1-5 ___, Continued

2.

	ASSETS				= LIABILITIES +	OWNER'S EQUITY									
	Cash	+ Accts. Rec.	+ Supplies	+ Land	= Accts. Payable	+ ______, Capital	– ______, Drawing	+ Dry Cleaning Revenue	– Dry Cleaning Exp.	– Wages Exp.	– Rent Exp.	– Supp. Exp.	– Truck Exp.	– Util. Exp.	– Misc. Exp.
Bal.															
a.															
Bal.															
b.															
Bal.															
c.															
Bal.															
d.															
Bal.															
e.															
Bal.															
f.															
Bal.															
g.															
Bal.															
h.															
Bal.															
i.															
Bal.															
j.															
Bal.															
k.															
Bal.															
l.															
Bal.															

PROBLEM 1-5 ___, Continued

3.

Income Statement

Statement of Owner's Equity

PROBLEM 1-5 ___, Continued

Balance Sheet

PROBLEM 1-5 ___, Concluded

4. (Optional)

Statement of Cash Flows

This Page Not Used.

PROBLEM 1-6 ___

a. ______________________________

____

b. ______________________________

____

c. ______________________________

____

d. ______________________________

____

e. ______________________________

____

f. ______________________________

____

g. ______________________________

____

h. ______________________________

____

i. ______________________________

____

j. ______________________________

____

k. ______________________________

____

l. ______________________________

____

m. ______________________________

____

n. ______________________________

____

o. ______________________________

____

p. ______________________________

____

q. ______________________________

____

This Page Not Used.

CONTINUING PROBLEM

1.

	Assets			= Liabilities +	Owner's Equity										
	Cash	+ Accts. Rec.	+ Supplies	= Accts. Pay.	+ Peyton Smith, Capital	– Peyton Smith, Drawing	+ Fees Earned	– Music Exp.	– Office Rent Exp.	– Equip. Rent Exp.	– Adv. Exp.	– Wages Exp.	– Util. Exp.	– Sup. Exp.	– Misc. Exp.
6/1															
6/2															
Bal.															
6/2															
Bal.															
6/4															
Bal.															
6/6															
Bal.															
6/8															
Bal.															
6/12															
Bal.															
6/13															
Bal.															
6/16															
Bal.															
6/22															
Bal.															
6/25															
Bal.															

CONTINUING PROBLEM, Continued

	ASSETS			= LIABILITIES +	OWNER'S EQUITY											
	Cash +	Accts. Rec. +	Supplies =	Accts. Pay. +	Peyton Smith, Capital –	Peyton Smith, Drawing +	Fees Earned –	Music Exp. –	Office Rent Exp. –	Equip. Rent Exp. –	Adv. Exp. –	Wages Exp. –	Util. Exp. –	Sup. Exp. –	Misc. Exp.
6/29															
Bal.															
6/30															
Bal.															
6/30															
Bal.															
6/30															
Bal.															
6/30															
Bal.															
6/30															
Bal.															
6/30															
Bal.															
6/30															
Bal.															

CONTINUING PROBLEM, Continued

2.

Income Statement

3.

Statement of Owner's Equity

CONTINUING PROBLEM, Concluded

4.

Balance Sheet

Name ______________________________

EXERCISE 2-1

Accounts Payable: ______________________________

Advanced Payments for Equipment: ______________________________

Air Traffic Liability: ______________________________

Aircraft Fuel (Expense): ______________________________

Aircraft Maintenance (Expense): ______________________________

Aircraft Rent (Expense): ______________________________

Cargo Revenue: ______________________________

Cash: ______________________________

Contract Carrier Arrangements (Expense): ______________________________

Flight Equipment: ______________________________

Frequent Flyer (Obligations): ______________________________

Fuel Inventory: ______________________________

Landing Fees (Expense): ______________________________

Parts and Supplies Inventories: ______________________________

Passenger Commissions (Expense): ______________________________

Passenger Revenue: ______________________________

Prepaid Expenses: ______________________________

Taxes Payable: ______________________________

EXERCISE 2-2

Account	Account Number
Accounts Payable..................	________
Accounts Receivable.............	________
Cash	________
Fees Earned..........................	________
Jackie Vargo, Capital	________
Jackie Vargo, Drawing	________
Land	________
Miscellaneous Expense	________
Supplies Expense	________
Wages Expense	________

EXERCISE 2-3

Balance Sheet Accounts

Acct. #	Account Name
	1. Assets
	2. Liabilities
	3. Owner's Equity

Income Statement Accounts

Acct. #	Account Name
	4. Revenue
	5. Expenses

EXERCISE 2-4

	Increase	Decrease	Normal Balance
Balance sheet accounts:			
Asset	(a) ________	(b) ________	Debit
Liability	(c) ________	Debit	(d) ________
Owner's Equity:			
Capital	Credit	(e) ________	(f) ________
Drawing	(g) ________	(h) ________	(i) ________
Income statement accounts:			
Revenue	(j) ________	(k) ________	Credit
Expense	(l) ________	Credit	Debit

EXERCISE 2-5

1. Accounts Payable: ______________________
2. Accounts Receivable: ______________________
3. Cash: ______________________
4. Fees Earned: ______________________
5. Insurance Expense: ______________________
6. Miriam Ramsey, Drawing: ______________________
7. Utilities Expense: ______________________

EXERCISE 2-6

a. Accounts Payable: ______________________
b. Accounts Receivable: ______________________
c. Bobby Lund, Capital: ______________________
d. Bobby Lund, Drawing: ______________________
e. Cash: ______________________
f. Fees Earned: ______________________
g. Office Equipment: ______________________
h. Rent Expense: ______________________
i. Supplies: ______________________
j. Wages Expense: ______________________

EXERCISE 2-7

JOURNAL

PAGE

	DATE		DESCRIPTION	POST. REF.	DEBIT	CREDIT	
1							1
2							2
3							3
4							4
5							5
6							6
7							7
8							8
9							9
10							10
11							11
12							12
13							13
14							14
15							15
16							16
17							17
18							18
19							19
20							20
21							21
22							22
23							23
24							24
25							25
26							26
27							27
28							28
29							29
30							30
31							31
32							32
33							33
34							34
35							35
36							36

EXERCISE 2-8

a.

JOURNAL PAGE 33

	DATE		DESCRIPTION	POST. REF.	DEBIT	CREDIT	
1							1
2							2
3							3
4							4
5							5

b., c., and d.

ACCOUNT ACCOUNT NO.

DATE		ITEM	POST. REF.	DEBIT	CREDIT	BALANCE	
						DEBIT	CREDIT

ACCOUNT ACCOUNT NO.

DATE		ITEM	POST. REF.	DEBIT	CREDIT	BALANCE	
						DEBIT	CREDIT

e. ____

EXERCISE 2-9

a.

JOURNAL PAGE

	DATE		DESCRIPTION	POST. REF.	DEBIT	CREDIT	
1							1
2							2
3							3
4							4
5							5
6							6
7							7
8							8
9							9
10							10
11							11

b.

Cash

Accounts Payable

Supplies

Fees Earned

Accounts Receivable

c. ______________________________

Name ______________________________

EXERCISE 2-10

a.

b.

EXERCISE 2-11

a.

Accounts Payable

b.

Accounts Receivable

EXERCISE 2-11, Concluded

c.

Cash	

EXERCISE 2-12

a.

b.

Name ______________________________

EXERCISE 2-13

a. and b.

	Account Debited		Account Credited	
Transaction	**Type**	**Effect**	**Type**	**Effect**
(1)	asset	+	owner's equity	+
(2)				
(3)				
(4)				
(5)				
(6)				
(7)				
(8)				
(9)				

EXERCISE 2-14

JOURNAL

PAGE

	DATE		DESCRIPTION	POST. REF.	DEBIT	CREDIT	
1							1
2							2
3							3
4							4
5							5
6							6
7							7
8							8
9							9
10							10
11							11
12							12
13							13
14							14
15							15
16							16
17							17
18							18
19							19
20							20
21							21
22							22
23							23
24							24
25							25
26							26
27							27
28							28
29							29
30							30
31							31
32							32
33							33
34							34
35							35
36							36

EXERCISE 2-15

a.

Unadjusted Trial Balance

---

b. ____

EXERCISE 2-16

Unadjusted Trial Balance

EXERCISE 2-17

EXERCISE 2-18

Unadjusted Trial Balance

EXERCISE 2-19

Error	(a) Out of Balance	(b) Difference	(c) Larger Total
1.	yes	$6,000	debit
2.			
3.			
4.			
5.			
6.			
7.			

EXERCISE 2-20

(Optional)

Unadjusted Trial Balance

Name ____________________

EXERCISE 2-21

JOURNAL PAGE

	DATE		DESCRIPTION	POST. REF.	DEBIT	CREDIT	
1							1
2							2
3							3
4							4
5							5
6							6
7							7
8							8
9							9

EXERCISE 2-22

JOURNAL PAGE

	DATE		DESCRIPTION	POST. REF.	DEBIT	CREDIT	
1							1
2							2
3							3
4							4
5							5
6							6
7							7
8							8
9							9
10							10

EXERCISE 2-23

a. **1.** Revenue: ____________________

2. Operating expenses: ____________________

3. Operating income: ____________________

b. ____________________

EXERCISE 2-24

a. 1. Revenue: ______________________

____

2. Operating expenses: ______________________

____

3. Operating income: ______________________

____

b. ______________________

____

____

____

____

c. ______________________

____

____

____

____

____

____

____

____

____

____

____

____

____

PROBLEM 2-1 ___

1. and 2.

Cash

Accounts Receivable

Supplies

Prepaid Insurance

Automobiles

PROBLEM 2-1 ___, Continued

Equipment

Notes Payable

Accounts Payable

__________________, *Capital*

Professional Fees

Rent Expense

PROBLEM 2-1 ___, Continued

Salary Expense

Blueprint Expense

Automobile Expense

Miscellaneous Expense

PROBLEM 2-1 ___, Concluded

3.

Unadjusted Trial Balance

4.

PROBLEM 2-2 ___

1.

JOURNAL

PAGE

	DATE		DESCRIPTION	POST. REF.	DEBIT	CREDIT	
1							1
2							2
3							3
4							4
5							5
6							6
7							7
8							8
9							9
10							10
11							11
12							12
13							13
14							14
15							15
16							16
17							17
18							18
19							19
20							20
21							21
22							22
23							23
24							24
25							25
26							26
27							27
28							28
29							29
30							30
31							31
32							32
33							33
34							34
35							35

PROBLEM 2-2 ___, Continued

2.

Cash

Supplies

Accounts Payable

______________________, *Capital*

______________________, *Drawing*

Sales Commissions

PROBLEM 2-2 ___, Continued

Rent Expense

Office Salaries Expense

Automobile Expense

Supplies Expense

Miscellaneous Expense

PROBLEM 2-2 ___, Concluded

3.

Unadjusted Trial Balance

4. a. ______________________________

b. ______________________________

c. ______________________________

5. ______________________________

____

PROBLEM 2-3 ___

1.

JOURNAL

PAGE *1*

	DATE		DESCRIPTION	POST. REF.	DEBIT	CREDIT	
1							1
2							2
3							3
4							4
5							5
6							6
7							7
8							8
9							9
10							10
11							11
12							12
13							13
14							14
15							15
16							16
17							17
18							18
19							19
20							20
21							21
22							22
23							23
24							24
25							25
26							26
27							27
28							28
29							29
30							30
31							31
32							32
33							33
34							34
35							35

PROBLEM 2-3 ___, Continued

JOURNAL

PAGE 2

DATE		DESCRIPTION	POST. REF.	DEBIT	CREDIT

PROBLEM 2-3 ___, Continued

2.

GENERAL LEDGER

ACCOUNT *Cash* ACCOUNT NO. *11*

DATE		ITEM	POST. REF.	DEBIT	CREDIT	BALANCE DEBIT	BALANCE CREDIT

ACCOUNT *Accounts Receivable* ACCOUNT NO. *12*

DATE		ITEM	POST. REF.	DEBIT	CREDIT	BALANCE DEBIT	BALANCE CREDIT

ACCOUNT *Supplies* ACCOUNT NO. *13*

DATE		ITEM	POST. REF.	DEBIT	CREDIT	BALANCE DEBIT	BALANCE CREDIT

ACCOUNT *Prepaid Insurance* ACCOUNT NO. *14*

DATE		ITEM	POST. REF.	DEBIT	CREDIT	BALANCE DEBIT	BALANCE CREDIT

PROBLEM 2-3 ___, Continued

ACCOUNT *Equipment* ACCOUNT NO. *16*

DATE		ITEM	POST. REF.	DEBIT	CREDIT	BALANCE	
						DEBIT	CREDIT

ACCOUNT *Truck* ACCOUNT NO. *18*

DATE		ITEM	POST. REF.	DEBIT	CREDIT	BALANCE	
						DEBIT	CREDIT

ACCOUNT *Notes Payable* ACCOUNT NO. *21*

DATE		ITEM	POST. REF.	DEBIT	CREDIT	BALANCE	
						DEBIT	CREDIT

ACCOUNT *Accounts Payable* ACCOUNT NO. *22*

DATE		ITEM	POST. REF.	DEBIT	CREDIT	BALANCE	
						DEBIT	CREDIT

ACCOUNT ______________________________, *Capital* ACCOUNT NO. *31*

DATE		ITEM	POST. REF.	DEBIT	CREDIT	BALANCE	
						DEBIT	CREDIT

PROBLEM 2-3 ___, Continued

ACCOUNT ______________________, *Drawing* ACCOUNT NO. *32*

DATE		ITEM	POST. REF.	DEBIT	CREDIT	BALANCE DEBIT	BALANCE CREDIT

ACCOUNT *Fees Earned* ACCOUNT NO. *41*

DATE		ITEM	POST. REF.	DEBIT	CREDIT	BALANCE DEBIT	BALANCE CREDIT

ACCOUNT *Wages Expense* ACCOUNT NO. *51*

DATE		ITEM	POST. REF.	DEBIT	CREDIT	BALANCE DEBIT	BALANCE CREDIT

ACCOUNT *Rent Expense* ACCOUNT NO. *53*

DATE		ITEM	POST. REF.	DEBIT	CREDIT	BALANCE DEBIT	BALANCE CREDIT

ACCOUNT *Utilities Expense* ACCOUNT NO. *54*

DATE		ITEM	POST. REF.	DEBIT	CREDIT	BALANCE DEBIT	BALANCE CREDIT

PROBLEM 2-3 ___, Continued

ACCOUNT *Truck Expense* ACCOUNT NO. *55*

DATE		ITEM	POST. REF.	DEBIT	CREDIT	BALANCE DEBIT	BALANCE CREDIT

ACCOUNT *Miscellaneous Expense* ACCOUNT NO. *59*

DATE		ITEM	POST. REF.	DEBIT	CREDIT	BALANCE DEBIT	BALANCE CREDIT

PROBLEM 2-3 ___, Concluded

3.

Unadjusted Trial Balance

4. ______________________________

____

____

5. ______________________________

____

This Page Not Used.

PROBLEM 2-4 ___

2. and 3.

JOURNAL

PAGE *18*

	DATE		DESCRIPTION	POST. REF.	DEBIT	CREDIT	
1							1
2							2
3							3
4							4
5							5
6							6
7							7
8							8
9							9
10							10
11							11
12							12
13							13
14							14
15							15
16							16
17							17
18							18
19							19
20							20
21							21
22							22
23							23
24							24
25							25
26							26
27							27
28							28
29							29
30							30
31							31
32							32
33							33
34							34
35							35

PROBLEM 2-4 ___, Continued

JOURNAL

PAGE 19

	DATE		DESCRIPTION	POST. REF.	DEBIT	CREDIT	
1							1
2							2
3							3
4							4
5							5
6							6
7							7
8							8
9							9
10							10
11							11
12							12
13							13
14							14
15							15
16							16
17							17
18							18
19							19
20							20
21							21
22							22
23							23
24							24
25							25
26							26
27							27
28							28
29							29
30							30
31							31
32							32
33							33
34							34
35							35
36							36

PROBLEM 2-4 ___, Continued

1. and 3.

GENERAL LEDGER

ACCOUNT *Cash* ACCOUNT NO. *11*

DATE	ITEM	POST. REF.	DEBIT	CREDIT	BALANCE	
					DEBIT	CREDIT

ACCOUNT *Accounts Receivable* ACCOUNT NO. *12*

DATE	ITEM	POST. REF.	DEBIT	CREDIT	BALANCE	
					DEBIT	CREDIT

ACCOUNT *Prepaid Insurance* ACCOUNT NO. *13*

DATE	ITEM	POST. REF.	DEBIT	CREDIT	BALANCE	
					DEBIT	CREDIT

PROBLEM 2-4 ___, Continued

ACCOUNT *Office Supplies* ACCOUNT NO. *14*

DATE	ITEM	POST. REF.	DEBIT	CREDIT	BALANCE	
					DEBIT	CREDIT

ACCOUNT *Land* ACCOUNT NO. *16*

DATE	ITEM	POST. REF.	DEBIT	CREDIT	BALANCE	
					DEBIT	CREDIT

ACCOUNT *Accounts Payable* ACCOUNT NO. *21*

DATE	ITEM	POST. REF.	DEBIT	CREDIT	BALANCE	
					DEBIT	CREDIT

ACCOUNT *Unearned Rent* ACCOUNT NO. *22*

DATE	ITEM	POST. REF.	DEBIT	CREDIT	BALANCE	
					DEBIT	CREDIT

ACCOUNT *Notes Payable* ACCOUNT NO. *23*

DATE	ITEM	POST. REF.	DEBIT	CREDIT	BALANCE	
					DEBIT	CREDIT

PROBLEM 2-4 ___, Continued

ACCOUNT ______________________, *Capital* ACCOUNT NO. *31*

DATE		ITEM	POST. REF.	DEBIT	CREDIT	BALANCE DEBIT	BALANCE CREDIT

ACCOUNT ______________________, *Drawing* ACCOUNT NO. *32*

DATE		ITEM	POST. REF.	DEBIT	CREDIT	BALANCE DEBIT	BALANCE CREDIT

ACCOUNT *Fees Earned* ACCOUNT NO. *41*

DATE		ITEM	POST. REF.	DEBIT	CREDIT	BALANCE DEBIT	BALANCE CREDIT

ACCOUNT *Salary and Commission Expense* ACCOUNT NO. *51*

DATE		ITEM	POST. REF.	DEBIT	CREDIT	BALANCE DEBIT	BALANCE CREDIT

ACCOUNT *Rent Expense* ACCOUNT NO. *52*

DATE		ITEM	POST. REF.	DEBIT	CREDIT	BALANCE DEBIT	BALANCE CREDIT

PROBLEM 2-4 ___, Continued

ACCOUNT *Advertising Expense* ACCOUNT NO. 53

DATE		ITEM	POST. REF.	DEBIT	CREDIT	BALANCE	
						DEBIT	CREDIT

ACCOUNT *Automobile Expense* ACCOUNT NO. 54

DATE		ITEM	POST. REF.	DEBIT	CREDIT	BALANCE	
						DEBIT	CREDIT

ACCOUNT *Miscellaneous Expense* ACCOUNT NO. 59

DATE		ITEM	POST. REF.	DEBIT	CREDIT	BALANCE	
						DEBIT	CREDIT

PROBLEM 2-4 ___, Concluded

4.

Unadjusted Trial Balance

5. a. ______________________________

____

____

b.

JOURNAL PAGE

	DATE		DESCRIPTION	POST. REF.	DEBIT	CREDIT	
1							1
2							2
3							3
4							4

c. ______________________________

This Page Not Used.

Name ______________________________

PROBLEM 2-5 ___

1.

Corrected Unadjusted Trial Balance

	DEBIT BALANCES	CREDIT BALANCES
Cash		
Accounts Receivable		
Supplies		
Prepaid Insurance		
Equipment		
Notes Payable		
Accounts Payable		
____________________, *Capital*		
____________________, *Drawing*		
Fees Earned		
Wages Expense		
Rent Expense		
Advertising Expense		
Gas, Electricity, and Water Expense		
Miscellaneous Expense		

2. ____

This Page Not Used.

CONTINUING PROBLEM

2. and 3.

JOURNAL

PAGE 1

	DATE		DESCRIPTION	POST. REF.	DEBIT	CREDIT	
1							1
2							2
3							3
4							4
5							5
6							6
7							7
8							8
9							9
10							10
11							11
12							12
13							13
14							14
15							15
16							16
17							17
18							18
19							19
20							20
21							21
22							22
23							23
24							24
25							25
26							26
27							27
28							28
29							29
30							30
31							31
32							32
33							33
34							34
35							35

CONTINUING PROBLEM, Continued

JOURNAL

PAGE 2

	DATE		DESCRIPTION	POST. REF.	DEBIT	CREDIT	
1							1
2							2
3							3
4							4
5							5
6							6
7							7
8							8
9							9
10							10
11							11
12							12
13							13
14							14
15							15
16							16
17							17
18							18
19							19
20							20
21							21
22							22
23							23
24							24
25							25
26							26
27							27
28							28
29							29
30							30
31							31
32							32
33							33
34							34
35							35
36							36

CONTINUING PROBLEM, Continued

JOURNAL

PAGE 3

	DATE		DESCRIPTION	POST. REF.	DEBIT	CREDIT	
1							1
2							2
3							3
4							4
5							5
6							6
7							7
8							8
9							9
10							10
11							11
12							12
13							13
14							14
15							15
16							16
17							17
18							18
19							19
20							20
21							21
22							22
23							23
24							24
25							25
26							26
27							27
28							28
29							29
30							30
31							31
32							32
33							33
34							34
35							35
36							36

CONTINUING PROBLEM, Continued

1. and 3.

GENERAL LEDGER

ACCOUNT *Cash* ACCOUNT NO. *11*

DATE		ITEM	POST. REF.	DEBIT	CREDIT	BALANCE	
						DEBIT	CREDIT

CONTINUING PROBLEM, Continued

ACCOUNT *Accounts Receivable* ACCOUNT NO. *12*

DATE		ITEM	POST. REF.	DEBIT	CREDIT	BALANCE	
						DEBIT	CREDIT

ACCOUNT *Supplies* ACCOUNT NO. *14*

DATE		ITEM	POST. REF.	DEBIT	CREDIT	BALANCE	
						DEBIT	CREDIT

ACCOUNT *Prepaid Insurance* ACCOUNT NO. *15*

DATE		ITEM	POST. REF.	DEBIT	CREDIT	BALANCE	
						DEBIT	CREDIT

ACCOUNT *Office Equipment* ACCOUNT NO. *17*

DATE		ITEM	POST. REF.	DEBIT	CREDIT	BALANCE	
						DEBIT	CREDIT

CONTINUING PROBLEM, Continued

ACCOUNT *Accumulated Depreciation—Office Equipment* ACCOUNT NO. *18*

DATE		ITEM	POST. REF.	DEBIT	CREDIT	BALANCE	
						DEBIT	CREDIT

(This account is not used in Chapter 2.)

ACCOUNT *Accounts Payable* ACCOUNT NO. *21*

DATE		ITEM	POST. REF.	DEBIT	CREDIT	BALANCE	
						DEBIT	CREDIT

ACCOUNT *Wages Payable* ACCOUNT NO. *22*

DATE		ITEM	POST. REF.	DEBIT	CREDIT	BALANCE	
						DEBIT	CREDIT

(This account is not used in Chapter 2.)

ACCOUNT *Unearned Revenue* ACCOUNT NO. *23*

DATE		ITEM	POST. REF.	DEBIT	CREDIT	BALANCE	
						DEBIT	CREDIT

CONTINUING PROBLEM, Continued

ACCOUNT *Peyton Smith, Capital* ACCOUNT NO. *31*

DATE		ITEM	POST. REF.	DEBIT	CREDIT	BALANCE	
						DEBIT	CREDIT

ACCOUNT *Peyton Smith, Drawing* ACCOUNT NO. *32*

DATE		ITEM	POST. REF.	DEBIT	CREDIT	BALANCE	
						DEBIT	CREDIT

ACCOUNT *Income Summary* ACCOUNT NO. *33*

DATE		ITEM	POST. REF.	DEBIT	CREDIT	BALANCE	
						DEBIT	CREDIT

(This account is not used in Chapter 2.)

CONTINUING PROBLEM, Continued

ACCOUNT *Fees Earned* ACCOUNT NO. *41*

DATE		ITEM	POST. REF.	DEBIT	CREDIT	BALANCE DEBIT	BALANCE CREDIT

ACCOUNT *Wages Expense* ACCOUNT NO. *50*

DATE		ITEM	POST. REF.	DEBIT	CREDIT	BALANCE DEBIT	BALANCE CREDIT

ACCOUNT *Office Rent Expense* ACCOUNT NO. *51*

DATE		ITEM	POST. REF.	DEBIT	CREDIT	BALANCE DEBIT	BALANCE CREDIT

CONTINUING PROBLEM, Continued

ACCOUNT *Equipment Rent Expense* ACCOUNT NO. *52*

DATE		ITEM	POST. REF.	DEBIT	CREDIT	BALANCE	
						DEBIT	CREDIT

ACCOUNT *Utilities Expense* ACCOUNT NO. *53*

DATE		ITEM	POST. REF.	DEBIT	CREDIT	BALANCE	
						DEBIT	CREDIT

ACCOUNT *Music Expense* ACCOUNT NO. *54*

DATE		ITEM	POST. REF.	DEBIT	CREDIT	BALANCE	
						DEBIT	CREDIT

ACCOUNT *Advertising Expense* ACCOUNT NO. *55*

DATE		ITEM	POST. REF.	DEBIT	CREDIT	BALANCE	
						DEBIT	CREDIT

CONTINUING PROBLEM, Continued

ACCOUNT *Supplies Expense* ACCOUNT NO. *56*

DATE		ITEM	POST. REF.	DEBIT	CREDIT	BALANCE DEBIT	BALANCE CREDIT

ACCOUNT *Insurance Expense* ACCOUNT NO. *57*

DATE		ITEM	POST. REF.	DEBIT	CREDIT	BALANCE DEBIT	BALANCE CREDIT

(This account is not used in Chapter 2.)

ACCOUNT *Depreciation Expense* ACCOUNT NO. *58*

DATE		ITEM	POST. REF.	DEBIT	CREDIT	BALANCE DEBIT	BALANCE CREDIT

(This account is not used in Chapter 2.)

ACCOUNT *Miscellaneous Expense* ACCOUNT NO. *59*

DATE		ITEM	POST. REF.	DEBIT	CREDIT	BALANCE DEBIT	BALANCE CREDIT

CONTINUING PROBLEM, Concluded

4.

Unadjusted Trial Balance

This Page Not Used.

EXERCISE 3-1

1. A two-year premium paid on a fire insurance policy: ______________________
2. Fees earned but not yet received: ______________________
3. Fees received but not yet earned: ______________________
4. Salary owed but not yet paid: ______________________
5. Subscriptions received in advance by a magazine publisher: ______________________
6. Supplies on hand: ______________________
7. Taxes owed but payable in the following period: ______________________
8. Utilities owed but not yet paid: ______________________

EXERCISE 3-2

Account	Answer
Accounts Receivable	Normally requires adjustment (AR).
Cash..	
Interest Expense	
Interest Receivable	
Johann Atkins, Capital	
Land	
Office Equipment	
Prepaid Rent	
Supplies	
Unearned Fees	
Wages Expense	

EXERCISE 3-3

JOURNAL PAGE

	DATE		DESCRIPTION	POST. REF.	DEBIT	CREDIT	
1							1
2							2
3							3
4							4

EXERCISE 3-4

____

____

EXERCISE 3-5

a. ____

____

____

b. ____

____

____

EXERCISE 3-6

a. and b.

JOURNAL PAGE

	DATE		DESCRIPTION	POST. REF.	DEBIT	CREDIT	
1							1
2							2
3							3
4							4
5							5
6							6
7							7

EXERCISE 3-7

a. and b.

JOURNAL PAGE

	DATE		DESCRIPTION	POST. REF.	DEBIT	CREDIT	
1							1
2							2
3							3
4							4
5							5
6							6
7							7

EXERCISE 3-8

JOURNAL PAGE

	DATE		DESCRIPTION	POST. REF.	DEBIT	CREDIT	
1							1
2							2
3							3

EXERCISE 3-9

a. ______________________

b. ______________________

EXERCISE 3-10

a.

JOURNAL PAGE

	DATE		DESCRIPTION	POST. REF.	DEBIT	CREDIT	
1							1
2							2
3							3

b. ______________________

EXERCISE 3-11

a. and b.

JOURNAL PAGE

	DATE		DESCRIPTION	POST. REF.	DEBIT	CREDIT	
1							1
2							2
3							3
4							4
5							5
6							6
7							7

EXERCISE 3-12

a. ____

____

b. ____

____

EXERCISE 3-13

a. and b.

JOURNAL PAGE

	DATE		DESCRIPTION	POST. REF.	DEBIT	CREDIT	
1							1
2							2
3							3
4							4
5							5
6							6
7							7
8							8
9							9

EXERCISE 3-14

____

____

____

EXERCISE 3-15

a. ______________________

b. ______________________

EXERCISE 3-16

a. ______________________

b. ______________________

EXERCISE 3-17

a.

JOURNAL PAGE

	DATE		DESCRIPTION	POST. REF.	DEBIT	CREDIT	
1							1
2							2
3							3
4							4
5							5
6							6
7							7
8							8

b. ______________________

EXERCISE 3-18

JOURNAL PAGE

	DATE		DESCRIPTION	POST. REF.	DEBIT	CREDIT	
1							1
2							2
3							3
4							4

EXERCISE 3-19

a. ______________________

b. ______________________

EXERCISE 3-20

a. ______________________

b. ______________________

EXERCISE 3-21

____

EXERCISE 3-22

a. ______________________

b. ______________________

EXERCISE 3-23

	Error (a)		Error (b)	
	Overstated	Understated	Overstated	Understated
1. Revenue for the year would be	$	$	$	$
2. Expenses for the year would be	$	$	$	$
3. Net income for the year would be	$	$	$	$
4. Assets at July 31 would be	$	$	$	$
5. Liabilities at July 31 would be	$	$	$	$
6. Owner's equity at July 31 would be	$	$	$	$

EXERCISE 3-24

____

____

EXERCISE 3-25

a.

JOURNAL PAGE

	DATE		DESCRIPTION	POST. REF.	DEBIT	CREDIT	
1							1
2							2
3							3
4							4

b. (1) ____

____

____

(2) ____

____

____

EXERCISE 3-26

JOURNAL

PAGE

	DATE		DESCRIPTION	POST. REF.	DEBIT	CREDIT	
1							1
2							2
3							3
4							4
5							5
6							6
7							7
8							8
9							9
10							10
11							11
12							12
13							13
14							14
15							15
16							16
17							17
18							18
19							19
20							20

EXERCISE 3-27

EXERCISE 3-27, Concluded

(Optional)

Adjusted Trial Balance

Name ______________________

EXERCISE 3-28

a.

b.

c.

EXERCISE 3-29

a. Dell Inc.

	AMOUNT	PERCENT

b. Hewlett-Packard Company (HP)

	AMOUNT	PERCENT

c.

This Page Not Used.

PROBLEM 3-1 ___

1.

JOURNAL

PAGE

	DATE		DESCRIPTION	POST. REF.	DEBIT	CREDIT	
1							1
2							2
3							3
4							4
5							5
6							6
7							7
8							8
9							9
10							10
11							11
12							12
13							13
14							14
15							15
16							16
17							17
18							18
19							19
20							20
21							21
22							22

2. ____

This Page Not Used.

PROBLEM 3-2 ___

1.

JOURNAL

PAGE

DATE		DESCRIPTION	POST. REF.	DEBIT	CREDIT

PROBLEM 3-2 ___, Concluded

2. ____

____

____

____

3. ____

____

____

____

____

____

____

____

4. ____

____

____

____

Name ______________________________

PROBLEM 3-3 ___

1.

JOURNAL

PAGE ______

DATE		DESCRIPTION	POST. REF.	DEBIT	CREDIT

PROBLEM 3-3 ___, Concluded

2.

	AMOUNT

3.

	AMOUNT

4. ____

____

____

____

Name ______________________________

PROBLEM 3-4 ___

JOURNAL

PAGE

DATE		DESCRIPTION	POST. REF.	DEBIT	CREDIT

This Page Not Used.

PROBLEM 3-5 ___

1.

JOURNAL

PAGE

	DATE		DESCRIPTION	POST. REF.	DEBIT	CREDIT	
1							1
2							2
3							3
4							4
5							5
6							6
7							7
8							8
9							9
10							10
11							11
12							12
13							13
14							14
15							15
16							16
17							17
18							18
19							19
20							20
21							21
22							22
23							23
24							24
25							25
26							26
27							27
28							28
29							29
30							30
31							31
32							32
33							33
34							34
35							35

PROBLEM 3-5 ___, Concluded

2.

Adjusted Trial Balance

Name ______________________________

PROBLEM 3-6 ___

1.

JOURNAL PAGE

	DATE		DESCRIPTION	POST. REF.	DEBIT	CREDIT	
1							1
2							2
3							3
4							4
5							5
6							6
7							7
8							8
9							9
10							10
11							11
12							12
13							13
14							14
15							15
16							16
17							17
18							18
19							19
20							20

2.

	Net Income	Total Assets	=	Total Liabilities	+	Total Owner's Equity
Reported amounts	$	$		$		$
Corrections:						
Adjustment (a)						
Adjustment (b)						
Adjustment (c)						
Adjustment (d)						
Corrected amounts	$	$		$		$

This Page Not Used.

Name ______________________________

CONTINUING PROBLEM

1.

JOURNAL

PAGE *3*

DATE		DESCRIPTION	POST. REF.	DEBIT	CREDIT

CONTINUING PROBLEM, Continued

2.

GENERAL LEDGER

ACCOUNT *Cash* ACCOUNT NO. *11*

DATE		ITEM	POST. REF.	DEBIT	CREDIT	BALANCE	
						DEBIT	CREDIT

CONTINUING PROBLEM, Continued

ACCOUNT *Accounts Receivable* ACCOUNT NO. *12*

DATE		ITEM	POST. REF.	DEBIT	CREDIT	BALANCE DEBIT	BALANCE CREDIT

ACCOUNT *Supplies* ACCOUNT NO. *14*

DATE		ITEM	POST. REF.	DEBIT	CREDIT	BALANCE DEBIT	BALANCE CREDIT

ACCOUNT *Prepaid Insurance* ACCOUNT NO. *15*

DATE		ITEM	POST. REF.	DEBIT	CREDIT	BALANCE DEBIT	BALANCE CREDIT

ACCOUNT *Office Equipment* ACCOUNT NO. *17*

DATE		ITEM	POST. REF.	DEBIT	CREDIT	BALANCE DEBIT	BALANCE CREDIT

CONTINUING PROBLEM, Continued

ACCOUNT *Accumulated Depreciation—Office Equipment* ACCOUNT NO. *18*

DATE		ITEM	POST. REF.	DEBIT	CREDIT	BALANCE DEBIT	BALANCE CREDIT

ACCOUNT *Accounts Payable* ACCOUNT NO. *21*

DATE		ITEM	POST. REF.	DEBIT	CREDIT	BALANCE DEBIT	BALANCE CREDIT

ACCOUNT *Wages Payable* ACCOUNT NO. *22*

DATE		ITEM	POST. REF.	DEBIT	CREDIT	BALANCE DEBIT	BALANCE CREDIT

ACCOUNT *Unearned Revenue* ACCOUNT NO. *23*

DATE		ITEM	POST. REF.	DEBIT	CREDIT	BALANCE DEBIT	BALANCE CREDIT

CONTINUING PROBLEM, Continued

ACCOUNT *Peyton Smith, Capital* ACCOUNT NO. *31*

DATE		ITEM	POST. REF.	DEBIT	CREDIT	BALANCE	
						DEBIT	CREDIT

ACCOUNT *Peyton Smith, Drawing* ACCOUNT NO. *32*

DATE		ITEM	POST. REF.	DEBIT	CREDIT	BALANCE	
						DEBIT	CREDIT

ACCOUNT *Fees Earned* ACCOUNT NO. *41*

DATE		ITEM	POST. REF.	DEBIT	CREDIT	BALANCE	
						DEBIT	CREDIT

CONTINUING PROBLEM, Continued

ACCOUNT *Wages Expense* ACCOUNT NO. *50*

DATE		ITEM	POST. REF.	DEBIT	CREDIT	BALANCE	
						DEBIT	CREDIT

ACCOUNT *Office Rent Expense* ACCOUNT NO. *51*

DATE		ITEM	POST. REF.	DEBIT	CREDIT	BALANCE	
						DEBIT	CREDIT

ACCOUNT *Equipment Rent Expense* ACCOUNT NO. *52*

DATE		ITEM	POST. REF.	DEBIT	CREDIT	BALANCE	
						DEBIT	CREDIT

ACCOUNT *Utilities Expense* ACCOUNT NO. *53*

DATE		ITEM	POST. REF.	DEBIT	CREDIT	BALANCE	
						DEBIT	CREDIT

CONTINUING PROBLEM, Continued

ACCOUNT *Music Expense* ACCOUNT NO. *54*

DATE		ITEM	POST. REF.	DEBIT	CREDIT	BALANCE DEBIT	BALANCE CREDIT

ACCOUNT *Advertising Expense* ACCOUNT NO. *55*

DATE		ITEM	POST. REF.	DEBIT	CREDIT	BALANCE DEBIT	BALANCE CREDIT

ACCOUNT *Supplies Expense* ACCOUNT NO. *56*

DATE		ITEM	POST. REF.	DEBIT	CREDIT	BALANCE DEBIT	BALANCE CREDIT

ACCOUNT *Insurance Expense* ACCOUNT NO. *57*

DATE		ITEM	POST. REF.	DEBIT	CREDIT	BALANCE DEBIT	BALANCE CREDIT

CONTINUING PROBLEM, Continued

ACCOUNT *Depreciation Expense* ACCOUNT NO. *58*

DATE		ITEM	POST. REF.	DEBIT	CREDIT	BALANCE	
						DEBIT	CREDIT

ACCOUNT *Miscellaneous Expense* ACCOUNT NO. *59*

DATE		ITEM	POST. REF.	DEBIT	CREDIT	BALANCE	
						DEBIT	CREDIT

CONTINUING PROBLEM, Concluded

3.

Adjusted Trial Balance

This Page Not Used.

EXERCISE 4-1

1. Accounts Payable: ______________________
2. Accounts Receivable: ______________________
3. Cash: ______________________
4. Danny Reacher, Drawing: ______________________
5. Fees Earned: ______________________
6. Supplies: ______________________
7. Unearned Rent: ______________________
8. Utilities Expense: ______________________
9. Wages Expense: ______________________
10. Wages Payable: ______________________

EXERCISE 4-2

1. Accounts Receivable: ______________________
2. Equipment: ______________________
3. Fees Earned: ______________________
4. Insurance Expense: ______________________
5. Prepaid Advertising: ______________________
6. Prepaid Rent: ______________________
7. Rent Revenue: ______________________
8. Salary Expense: ______________________
9. Salary Payable: ______________________
10. Supplies: ______________________
11. Supplies Expense: ______________________
12. Unearned Rent: ______________________

EXERCISE 4-3

Income Statement

Statement of Owner's Equity

Name ______________________

EXERCISE 4-3, Concluded

Balance Sheet

EXERCISE 4-4

Income Statement

Statement of Owner's Equity

EXERCISE 4-4, Concluded

Balance Sheet

EXERCISE 4-5

Income Statement

EXERCISE 4-6

Income Statement

EXERCISE 4-7

a.

Income Statement

b. ______________________________

EXERCISE 4-8

Statement of Owner's Equity

EXERCISE 4-9

Statement of Owner's Equity

EXERCISE 4-10

1. Accounts receivable: ______________________
2. Building: ______________________
3. Cash: ______________________
4. Equipment: ______________________
5. Prepaid Insurance: ______________________
6. Supplies: ______________________

EXERCISE 4-11

Name ______________________

EXERCISE 4-12

Balance Sheet

EXERCISE 4-13

EXERCISE 4-13, Concluded

Balance Sheet

EXERCISE 4-14

a. Accounts Payable: ______________________

b. Accumulated Depreciation—Equipment: ______________________

c. Depreciation Expense—Equipment: ______________________

d. Equipment: ______________________

e. Ellen Drake, Capital: ______________________

f. Ellen Drake, Drawing: ______________________

g. Fees Earned: ______

h. Land: ______

i. Supplies: ______________________

j. Supplies Expense: ______________________

k. Wages Expense: ______________________

l. Wages Payable: ______________________

EXERCISE 4-15

____

____

____

____

____

____

____

EXERCISE 4-16

a.

JOURNAL PAGE

	DATE		DESCRIPTION	POST. REF.	DEBIT	CREDIT	
1							1
2							2
3							3
4							4
5							5
6							6

b. ______________________

Name ______________________________

EXERCISE 4-17

JOURNAL PAGE

	DATE		DESCRIPTION	POST. REF.	DEBIT	CREDIT	
1							1
2							2
3							3
4							4
5							5
6							6
7							7
8							8
9							9
10							10
11							11
12							12
13							13
14							14
15							15
16							16
17							17
18							18
19							19
20							20

EXERCISE 4-18

a. Accounts Payable: ______________________________

b. Accumulated Depreciation: ______________________________

c. Ben Crayton, Capital: ______________________________

d. Ben Crayton, Drawing: ______________________________

e. Cash: ______________________________

f. Depreciation Expense: ______________________________

g. Fees Earned: ______________________________

h. Office Equipment: ______________________________

i. Salaries Expense: ______________________________

j. Salaries Payable: ______________________________

k. Supplies: ______________________________

EXERCISE 4-19

Post-Closing Trial Balance

Name ______________________________

EXERCISE 4-20

1. ______________________________
2. ______________________________
3. ______________________________
4. ______________________________
5. ______________________________
6. ______________________________
7. ______________________________
8. ______________________________
9. ______________________________
10. ______________________________

EXERCISE 4-21

a.

	December 31	
	Year 2	**Year 1**
Current assets	$689,663	$558,850
Current liabilities	183,607	149,147
Working capital	________	________
Current ratio	________	________

b. ______________________________

EXERCISE 4-22

a.

	Year 2	**Year 1**
Current assets	$4,199,600	$3,794,900
Current liabilities	2,209,200	2,075,800
Working capital	________	________
Current ratio	________	________

b. ______________________________

APPENDIX EXERCISE 4-23

1. ______________________
2. ______________________
3. ______________________
4. ______________________
5. ______________________
6. ______________________
7. ______________________
8. ______________________
9. ______________________
10. ______________________

Name ______________________________

APPENDIX EXERCISE 4-24

	A	B	C	D	E	F	G	H	I	J	K
1	Alert Security Services Co.										
2	End-of-Period Spreadsheet (Work Sheet)										
3	For the Year Ended October 31, 2016										
4		Unadjusted				Adjusted		Income		Balance	
5		Trial Balance		Adjustments		Trial Balance		Statement		Sheet	
6	**Account Title**	Dr.	Cr.	Dr.	Cr.	Dr.	Cr.	Dr.	Cr.	Dr.	Cr.
7	Cash	12									
8	Accounts Receivable	90									
9	Supplies	8									
10	Prepaid Insurance	12									
11	Land	190									
12	Equipment	50									
13	Accumulated Depr.—Equip.		4								
14	Accounts Payable		36								
15	Wages Payable		0								
16	Brenda Schultz, Capital		260								
17	Brenda Schultz, Drawing	8									
18	Fees Earned		200								
19	Wages Expense	110									
20	Rent Expense	12									
21	Insurance Expense	0									
22	Utilities Expense	6									
23	Supplies Expense	0									
24	Depreciation Expense	0									
25	Miscellaneous Expense	2									
26	Totals	500	500								
27											
28											
29											
30											
31											

Name ______________________

APPENDIX EXERCISE 4-25

	A	B	C	D	E	F	G	H	I	J	K
1	Alert Security Services Co.										
2	End-of-Period Spreadsheet (Work Sheet)										
3	For the Year Ended October 31, 2016										
4		Unadjusted				Adjusted		Income		Balance	
5		Trial Balance		Adjustments		Trial Balance		Statement		Sheet	
6	**Account Title**	**Dr.**	**Cr.**	**Dr.**	**Cr.**	**Dr.**	**Cr.**	**Dr.**	**Cr.**	**Dr.**	**Cr.**
7	Cash					12					
8	Accounts Receivable					103					
9	Supplies					4					
10	Prepaid Insurance					2					
11	Land					190					
12	Equipment					50					
13	Accumulated Depr.—Equip.						7				
14	Accounts Payable						36				
15	Wages Payable						1				
16	Brenda Schultz, Capital						260				
17	Brenda Schultz, Drawing					8					
18	Fees Earned						213				
19	Wages Expense					111					
20	Rent Expense					12					
21	Insurance Expense					10					
22	Utilities Expense					6					
23	Supplies Expense					4					
24	Depreciation Expense					3					
25	Miscellaneous Expense					2					
26	Totals					517	517				
27	Net income (loss)										
28											
29											
30											
31											

APPENDIX EXERCISE 4-26

Income Statement

Statement of Owner's Equity

Name ______________________________

APPENDIX EXERCISE 4-26, Concluded

Balance Sheet

APPENDIX EXERCISE 4-27

JOURNAL

PAGE

	DATE		DESCRIPTION	POST. REF.	DEBIT	CREDIT	
1							1
2							2
3							3
4							4
5							5
6							6
7							7
8							8
9							9
10							10
11							11
12							12
13							13
14							14
15							15
16							16
17							17
18							18
19							19
20							20
21							21
22							22
23							23
24							24

APPENDIX EXERCISE 4-28

JOURNAL

PAGE

	DATE		DESCRIPTION	POST. REF.	DEBIT	CREDIT	
1							1
2							2
3							3
4							4
5							5
6							6
7							7
8							8
9							9
10							10
11							11
12							12
13							13
14							14
15							15
16							16
17							17
18							18
19							19
20							20
21							21
22							22
23							23
24							24

PROBLEM 4-1 ___

1.

Income Statement

2.

Statement of Owner's Equity

Name ______________________________

PROBLEM 4-1 ___, Continued

3.

Balance Sheet

PROBLEM 4-1 ___, Continued

4.

JOURNAL PAGE

	DATE		DESCRIPTION	POST. REF.	DEBIT	CREDIT	
1			*Closing Entries*				1
2							2
3							3
4							4
5							5
6							6
7							7
8							8
9							9
10							10
11							11
12							12
13							13
14							14
15							15
16							16
17							17
18							18
19							19
20							20
21							21
22							22
23							23
24							24
25							25
26							26
27							27
28							28
29							29
30							30
31							31
32							32
33							33
34							34
35							35

PROBLEM 4-1 ___, Concluded

5.

Post-Closing Trial Balance

PROBLEM 4-2 ___

1.

Income Statement

Statement of Owner's Equity

Name ______________________________

PROBLEM 4-2 ___, Continued

Balance Sheet

PROBLEM 4-2 ___, Concluded

2.

JOURNAL

PAGE

	DATE		DESCRIPTION	POST. REF.	DEBIT	CREDIT	
1			*Closing Entries*				1
2							2
3							3
4							4
5							5
6							6
7							7
8							8
9							9
10							10
11							11
12							12
13							13
14							14
15							15
16							16
17							17
18							18
19							19
20							20
21							21
22							22
23							23
24							24

3. ______________________

This Page Not Used.

PROBLEM 4-3 ___

1., 3., and 6.

Cash

Laundry Supplies

Prepaid Insurance

Laundry Equipment

Accumulated Depreciation

Accounts Payable

PROBLEM 4-3 ___, Continued

Wages Payable

________________________, Capital

________________________, Drawing

Income Summary

Laundry Revenue

Wages Expense

PROBLEM 4-3 ___, Continued

Rent Expense

Utilities Expense

Laundry Supplies Expense

Depreciation Expense

Insurance Expense

Miscellaneous Expense

PROBLEM 4-3 ___, Continued

2. Optional (Appendix)

	A	B	C	D	E	F	G	H	I	J	K
1											
2	End-of-Period Spreadsheet (Work Sheet)										
3											
4		Unadjusted				Adjusted		Income		Balance	
5		Trial Balance		Adjustments		Trial Balance		Statement		Sheet	
6	Account Title	Dr.	Cr.	Dr.	Cr.	Dr.	Cr.	Dr.	Cr.	Dr.	Cr.
7											
8											
9											
10											
11											
12											
13											
14											
15											
16											
17											
18											
19											
20											
21											
22											
23											
24											
25											
26											
27											
28											
29											
30											

PROBLEM 4-3 ___, Continued

3.

JOURNAL

PAGE

DATE		DESCRIPTION	POST. REF.	DEBIT	CREDIT
		Adjusting Entries			

PROBLEM 4-3 ___, Continued

4.

Adjusted Trial Balance

PROBLEM 4-3 ___, Continued

5.

Income Statement

Statement of Owner's Equity

Name ________________________

PROBLEM 4-3 ___, Continued

Balance Sheet

PROBLEM 4-3 ___, Continued

6.

JOURNAL

PAGE

	DATE		DESCRIPTION	POST. REF.	DEBIT	CREDIT	
1			*Closing Entries*				1
2							2
3							3
4							4
5							5
6							6
7							7
8							8
9							9
10							10
11							11
12							12
13							13
14							14
15							15
16							16
17							17
18							18
19							19
20							20
21							21
22							22
23							23
24							24
25							25
26							26
27							27
28							28
29							29
30							30
31							31
32							32
33							33
34							34
35							35

PROBLEM 4-3 ___, Concluded

7.

Post-Closing Trial Balance

Name ______________________

PROBLEM 4-4 ___

1., 3., and 6.

GENERAL LEDGER

ACCOUNT *Cash* ACCOUNT NO. *11*

DATE		ITEM	POST. REF.	DEBIT	CREDIT	BALANCE DEBIT	BALANCE CREDIT

ACCOUNT *Supplies* ACCOUNT NO. *13*

DATE		ITEM	POST. REF.	DEBIT	CREDIT	BALANCE DEBIT	BALANCE CREDIT

ACCOUNT *Prepaid Insurance* ACCOUNT NO. *14*

DATE		ITEM	POST. REF.	DEBIT	CREDIT	BALANCE DEBIT	BALANCE CREDIT

ACCOUNT *Equipment* ACCOUNT NO. *16*

DATE		ITEM	POST. REF.	DEBIT	CREDIT	BALANCE DEBIT	BALANCE CREDIT

ACCOUNT *Accumulated Depreciation—Equipment* ACCOUNT NO. *17*

DATE		ITEM	POST. REF.	DEBIT	CREDIT	BALANCE DEBIT	BALANCE CREDIT

PROBLEM 4-4 ___, Continued

ACCOUNT *Trucks* ACCOUNT NO. *18*

DATE		ITEM	POST. REF.	DEBIT	CREDIT	BALANCE	
						DEBIT	CREDIT

ACCOUNT *Accumulated Depreciation—Trucks* ACCOUNT NO. *19*

DATE		ITEM	POST. REF.	DEBIT	CREDIT	BALANCE	
						DEBIT	CREDIT

ACCOUNT *Accounts Payable* ACCOUNT NO. *21*

DATE		ITEM	POST. REF.	DEBIT	CREDIT	BALANCE	
						DEBIT	CREDIT

ACCOUNT *Wages Payable* ACCOUNT NO. *22*

DATE		ITEM	POST. REF.	DEBIT	CREDIT	BALANCE	
						DEBIT	CREDIT

ACCOUNT ______________________________*, Capital* ACCOUNT NO. *31*

DATE		ITEM	POST. REF.	DEBIT	CREDIT	BALANCE	
						DEBIT	CREDIT

PROBLEM 4-4 ___, Continued

ACCOUNT ______________________, *Drawing* ACCOUNT NO. *32*

DATE		ITEM	POST. REF.	DEBIT	CREDIT	BALANCE	
						DEBIT	CREDIT

ACCOUNT *Income Summary* ACCOUNT NO. *33*

DATE		ITEM	POST. REF.	DEBIT	CREDIT	BALANCE	
						DEBIT	CREDIT

ACCOUNT *Service Revenue* ACCOUNT NO. *41*

DATE		ITEM	POST. REF.	DEBIT	CREDIT	BALANCE	
						DEBIT	CREDIT

ACCOUNT *Wages Expense* ACCOUNT NO. *51*

DATE		ITEM	POST. REF.	DEBIT	CREDIT	BALANCE	
						DEBIT	CREDIT

PROBLEM 4-4 ___, Continued

ACCOUNT *Supplies Expense* ACCOUNT NO.

DATE		ITEM	POST. REF.	DEBIT	CREDIT	BALANCE	
						DEBIT	CREDIT

ACCOUNT *Rent Expense* ACCOUNT NO.

DATE		ITEM	POST. REF.	DEBIT	CREDIT	BALANCE	
						DEBIT	CREDIT

ACCOUNT *Depreciation Expense—Equipment* ACCOUNT NO.

DATE		ITEM	POST. REF.	DEBIT	CREDIT	BALANCE	
						DEBIT	CREDIT

ACCOUNT *Truck Expense* ACCOUNT NO.

DATE		ITEM	POST. REF.	DEBIT	CREDIT	BALANCE	
						DEBIT	CREDIT

ACCOUNT *Depreciation Expense—Trucks* ACCOUNT NO. *56*

DATE		ITEM	POST. REF.	DEBIT	CREDIT	BALANCE	
						DEBIT	CREDIT

Name ______________________________

PROBLEM 4-4 ___, Continued

ACCOUNT *Insurance Expense* ACCOUNT NO. *57*

DATE		ITEM	POST. REF.	DEBIT	CREDIT	BALANCE DEBIT	BALANCE CREDIT

ACCOUNT *Miscellaneous Expense* ACCOUNT NO. *59*

DATE		ITEM	POST. REF.	DEBIT	CREDIT	BALANCE DEBIT	BALANCE CREDIT

Name ______________________________

PROBLEM 4-4 ___, Continued

2. Optional (Appendix)

	A	B	C	D	E	F	G	H	I	J	K
1											
2	End-of-Period Spreadsheet (Work Sheet)										
3											
4		Unadjusted				Adjusted		Income		Balance	
5		Trial Balance		Adjustments		Trial Balance		Statement		Sheet	
6	Account Title	Dr.	Cr.	Dr.	Cr.	Dr.	Cr.	Dr.	Cr.	Dr.	Cr.
7											
8											
9											
10											
11											
12											
13											
14											
15											
16											
17											
18											
19											
20											
21											
22											
23											
24											
25											
26											
27											
28											
29											
30											

PROBLEM 4-4 ___, Continued

3.

JOURNAL

PAGE *26*

DATE		DESCRIPTION	POST. REF.	DEBIT	CREDIT
		Adjusting Entries			

PROBLEM 4-4 ___, Continued

4.

Adjusted Trial Balance

PROBLEM 4-4 ___, Continued

5.

Income Statement

Statement of Owner's Equity

Name ____________________

PROBLEM 4-4 ___, Continued

Balance Sheet

Name ______________________________

PROBLEM 4-4 ___, Continued

6.

JOURNAL PAGE *27*

DATE		DESCRIPTION	POST. REF.	DEBIT	CREDIT
		Closing Entries			

PROBLEM 4-4 ___, Concluded

7.

Post-Closing Trial Balance

PROBLEM 4-5 ___

1. and 2.

JOURNAL

PAGE *1*

	DATE		DESCRIPTION	POST. REF.	DEBIT	CREDIT	
1							1
2							2
3							3
4							4
5							5
6							6
7							7
8							8
9							9
10							10
11							11
12							12
13							13
14							14
15							15
16							16
17							17
18							18
19							19
20							20
21							21
22							22
23							23
24							24
25							25
26							26
27							27
28							28
29							29
30							30
31							31
32							32
33							33
34							34
35							35

PROBLEM 4-5 ___, Continued

JOURNAL

PAGE 2

	DATE		DESCRIPTION	POST. REF.	DEBIT	CREDIT	
1							1
2							2
3							3
4							4
5							5
6							6
7							7
8							8
9							9
10							10
11							11
12							12
13							13
14							14
15							15
16							16
17							17
18							18
19							19
20							20
21							21
22							22
23							23
24							24
25							25
26							26
27							27
28							28
29							29
30							30
31							31
32							32
33							33
34							34
35							35
36							36

PROBLEM 4-5 ___, Continued

2., 6., and 9.

GENERAL LEDGER

ACCOUNT *Cash* ACCOUNT NO. *11*

DATE		ITEM	POST. REF.	DEBIT	CREDIT	BALANCE DEBIT	BALANCE CREDIT

ACCOUNT *Accounts Receivable* ACCOUNT NO. *12*

DATE		ITEM	POST. REF.	DEBIT	CREDIT	BALANCE DEBIT	BALANCE CREDIT

PROBLEM 4-5 ___, Continued

ACCOUNT *Supplies* ACCOUNT NO. *14*

DATE		ITEM	POST. REF.	DEBIT	CREDIT	BALANCE	
						DEBIT	CREDIT

ACCOUNT *Prepaid Rent* ACCOUNT NO. *15*

DATE		ITEM	POST. REF.	DEBIT	CREDIT	BALANCE	
						DEBIT	CREDIT

ACCOUNT *Prepaid Insurance* ACCOUNT NO. *16*

DATE		ITEM	POST. REF.	DEBIT	CREDIT	BALANCE	
						DEBIT	CREDIT

ACCOUNT *Office Equipment* ACCOUNT NO. *18*

DATE		ITEM	POST. REF.	DEBIT	CREDIT	BALANCE	
						DEBIT	CREDIT

ACCOUNT *Accumulated Depreciation* ACCOUNT NO. *19*

DATE		ITEM	POST. REF.	DEBIT	CREDIT	BALANCE	
						DEBIT	CREDIT

PROBLEM 4-5 ___, Continued

ACCOUNT *Accounts Payable* ACCOUNT NO. *21*

DATE		ITEM	POST. REF.	DEBIT	CREDIT	BALANCE DEBIT	BALANCE CREDIT

ACCOUNT *Salaries Payable* ACCOUNT NO. *22*

DATE		ITEM	POST. REF.	DEBIT	CREDIT	BALANCE DEBIT	BALANCE CREDIT

ACCOUNT *Unearned Fees* ACCOUNT NO. *23*

DATE		ITEM	POST. REF.	DEBIT	CREDIT	BALANCE DEBIT	BALANCE CREDIT

ACCOUNT ______________________________, *Capital* ACCOUNT NO. *31*

DATE		ITEM	POST. REF.	DEBIT	CREDIT	BALANCE DEBIT	BALANCE CREDIT

ACCOUNT ______________________________, *Drawing* ACCOUNT NO. *32*

DATE		ITEM	POST. REF.	DEBIT	CREDIT	BALANCE DEBIT	BALANCE CREDIT

PROBLEM 4-5 ___, Continued

ACCOUNT *Income Summary* ACCOUNT NO. *33*

DATE	ITEM	POST. REF.	DEBIT	CREDIT	BALANCE	
					DEBIT	CREDIT

ACCOUNT *Fees Earned* ACCOUNT NO. *41*

DATE	ITEM	POST. REF.	DEBIT	CREDIT	BALANCE	
					DEBIT	CREDIT

ACCOUNT *Salary Expense* ACCOUNT NO. *51*

DATE	ITEM	POST. REF.	DEBIT	CREDIT	BALANCE	
					DEBIT	CREDIT

ACCOUNT *Rent Expense* ACCOUNT NO.

DATE	ITEM	POST. REF.	DEBIT	CREDIT	BALANCE	
					DEBIT	CREDIT

PROBLEM 4-5 ___, Continued

ACCOUNT *Supplies Expense* ACCOUNT NO.

DATE		ITEM	POST. REF.	DEBIT	CREDIT	BALANCE DEBIT	BALANCE CREDIT

ACCOUNT *Depreciation Expense* ACCOUNT NO. *54*

DATE		ITEM	POST. REF.	DEBIT	CREDIT	BALANCE DEBIT	BALANCE CREDIT

ACCOUNT *Insurance Expense* ACCOUNT NO. *55*

DATE		ITEM	POST. REF.	DEBIT	CREDIT	BALANCE DEBIT	BALANCE CREDIT

ACCOUNT *Miscellaneous Expense* ACCOUNT NO. *59*

DATE		ITEM	POST. REF.	DEBIT	CREDIT	BALANCE DEBIT	BALANCE CREDIT

PROBLEM 4-5 ___, Continued

3.

Unadjusted Trial Balance

PROBLEM 4-5 ___, Continued

5. Optional (Appendix)

	A	B	C	D	E	F	G	H	I	J	K
1											
2	**End-of-Period Spreadsheet (Work Sheet)**										
3											
4		**Unadjusted Trial Balance**		**Adjustments**		**Adjusted Trial Balance**		**Income Statement**		**Balance Sheet**	
5											
6	**Account Title**	**Dr.**	**Cr.**	**Dr.**	**Cr.**	**Dr.**	**Cr.**	**Dr.**	**Cr.**	**Dr.**	**Cr.**
7											
8											
9											
10											
11											
12											
13											
14											
15											
16											
17											
18											
19											
20											
21											
22											
23											
24											
25											
26											
27											
28											
29											
30											

PROBLEM 4-5 ___, Continued

6.

JOURNAL

PAGE *3*

	DATE		DESCRIPTION	POST. REF.	DEBIT	CREDIT	
1			*Adjusting Entries*				1
2							2
3							3
4							4
5							5
6							6
7							7
8							8
9							9
10							10
11							11
12							12
13							13
14							14
15							15
16							16
17							17
18							18
19							19
20							20
21							21
22							22
23							23
24							24
25							25
26							26
27							27
28							28
29							29
30							30
31							31
32							32
33							33
34							34
35							35

PROBLEM 4-5 ___, Continued

7.

Adjusted Trial Balance

PROBLEM 4-5 ___, Continued

8.

Income Statement

Statement of Owner's Equity

Name ____________________

PROBLEM 4-5 ___, Continued

Balance Sheet

PROBLEM 4-5 ___, Continued

9.

JOURNAL

PAGE *4*

	DATE		DESCRIPTION	POST. REF.	DEBIT	CREDIT	
1			*Closing Entries*				1
2							2
3							3
4							4
5							5
6							6
7							7
8							8
9							9
10							10
11							11
12							12
13							13
14							14
15							15
16							16
17							17
18							18
19							19
20							20
21							21
22							22
23							23
24							24
25							25
26							26
27							27
28							28
29							29
30							30
31							31
32							32
33							33
34							34
35							35

PROBLEM 4-5 ___, Concluded

10.

Post-Closing Trial Balance

This Page Not Used.

CONTINUING PROBLEM

1. Optional (Appendix)

	A	B	C	D	E	F	G	H	I	J	K
1											
2	End-of-Period Spreadsheet (Work Sheet)										
3											
4		Unadjusted				Adjusted		Income		Balance	
5		Trial Balance		Adjustments		Trial Balance		Statement		Sheet	
6	Account Title	Dr.	Cr.	Dr.	Cr.	Dr.	Cr.	Dr.	Cr.	Dr.	Cr.
7											
8											
9											
10											
11											
12											
13											
14											
15											
16											
17											
18											
19											
20											
21											
22											
23											
24											
25											
26											
27											
28											
29											
30											
31											
32											

CONTINUING PROBLEM, Continued

2.

Income Statement

Statement of Owner's Equity

CONTINUING PROBLEM, Continued

Balance Sheet

CONTINUING PROBLEM, Continued

3. Note: Use the general ledger accounts provided in Chapter 3, page 116–122.

JOURNAL

PAGE *4*

	DATE		DESCRIPTION	POST. REF.	DEBIT	CREDIT	
1			*Closing Entries*				1
2							2
3							3
4							4
5							5
6							6
7							7
8							8
9							9
10							10
11							11
12							12
13							13
14							14
15							15
16							16
17							17
18							18
19							19
20							20
21							21
22							22
23							23
24							24
25							25
26							26
27							27
28							28
29							29
30							30
31							31
32							32
33							33
34							34

Name ______________________________

CONTINUING PROBLEM, Concluded

4.

Post-Closing Trial Balance

This Page Not Used.

COMPREHENSIVE PROBLEM 1

1. and 2.

JOURNAL

PAGE 5

DATE		DESCRIPTION	POST. REF.	DEBIT	CREDIT

COMPREHENSIVE PROBLEM 1, Continued

JOURNAL

PAGE 6

	DATE		DESCRIPTION	POST. REF.	DEBIT	CREDIT	
1							1
2							2
3							3
4							4
5							5
6							6
7							7
8							8
9							9
10							10
11							11
12							12
13							13
14							14
15							15
16							16
17							17
18							18
19							19
20							20
21							21
22							22
23							23
24							24
25							25
26							26
27							27
28							28
29							29
30							30
31							31
32							32
33							33
34							34
35							35

Name ______________________________

COMPREHENSIVE PROBLEM 1, Continued

2., 6., and 9.

GENERAL LEDGER

ACCOUNT *Cash* ACCOUNT NO. *11*

DATE		ITEM	POST. REF.	DEBIT	CREDIT	BALANCE	
						DEBIT	CREDIT

ACCOUNT *Accounts Receivable* ACCOUNT NO. *12*

DATE		ITEM	POST. REF.	DEBIT	CREDIT	BALANCE	
						DEBIT	CREDIT

COMPREHENSIVE PROBLEM 1, Continued

ACCOUNT *Supplies* ACCOUNT NO. *14*

DATE		ITEM	POST. REF.	DEBIT	CREDIT	BALANCE DEBIT	BALANCE CREDIT

ACCOUNT *Prepaid Rent* ACCOUNT NO. *15*

DATE		ITEM	POST. REF.	DEBIT	CREDIT	BALANCE DEBIT	BALANCE CREDIT

ACCOUNT *Prepaid Insurance* ACCOUNT NO. *16*

DATE		ITEM	POST. REF.	DEBIT	CREDIT	BALANCE DEBIT	BALANCE CREDIT

ACCOUNT *Office Equipment* ACCOUNT NO. *18*

DATE		ITEM	POST. REF.	DEBIT	CREDIT	BALANCE DEBIT	BALANCE CREDIT

ACCOUNT *Accumulated Depreciation* ACCOUNT NO. *19*

DATE		ITEM	POST. REF.	DEBIT	CREDIT	BALANCE DEBIT	BALANCE CREDIT

Name ______________________________

COMPREHENSIVE PROBLEM 1, Continued

ACCOUNT *Accounts Payable* ACCOUNT NO. *21*

DATE		ITEM	POST. REF.	DEBIT	CREDIT	BALANCE DEBIT	BALANCE CREDIT

ACCOUNT *Salaries Payable* ACCOUNT NO. *22*

DATE		ITEM	POST. REF.	DEBIT	CREDIT	BALANCE DEBIT	BALANCE CREDIT

ACCOUNT *Unearned Fees* ACCOUNT NO. *23*

DATE		ITEM	POST. REF.	DEBIT	CREDIT	BALANCE DEBIT	BALANCE CREDIT

ACCOUNT *Kelly Pitney, Capital* ACCOUNT NO. *31*

DATE		ITEM	POST. REF.	DEBIT	CREDIT	BALANCE DEBIT	BALANCE CREDIT

COMPREHENSIVE PROBLEM 1, Continued

ACCOUNT *Kelly Pitney, Drawing* ACCOUNT NO. *32*

DATE		ITEM	POST. REF.	DEBIT	CREDIT	BALANCE	
						DEBIT	CREDIT

ACCOUNT *Income Summary* ACCOUNT NO. *33*

DATE		ITEM	POST. REF.	DEBIT	CREDIT	BALANCE	
						DEBIT	CREDIT

ACCOUNT *Fees Earned* ACCOUNT NO. *41*

DATE		ITEM	POST. REF.	DEBIT	CREDIT	BALANCE	
						DEBIT	CREDIT

ACCOUNT *Salary Expense* ACCOUNT NO. *51*

DATE		ITEM	POST. REF.	DEBIT	CREDIT	BALANCE	
						DEBIT	CREDIT

COMPREHENSIVE PROBLEM 1, Continued

ACCOUNT *Rent Expense* ACCOUNT NO. *52*

DATE		ITEM	POST. REF.	DEBIT	CREDIT	BALANCE DEBIT	BALANCE CREDIT

ACCOUNT *Supplies Expense* ACCOUNT NO. *53*

DATE		ITEM	POST. REF.	DEBIT	CREDIT	BALANCE DEBIT	BALANCE CREDIT

ACCOUNT *Depreciation Expense* ACCOUNT NO. *54*

DATE		ITEM	POST. REF.	DEBIT	CREDIT	BALANCE DEBIT	BALANCE CREDIT

ACCOUNT *Insurance Expense* ACCOUNT NO. *55*

DATE		ITEM	POST. REF.	DEBIT	CREDIT	BALANCE DEBIT	BALANCE CREDIT

COMPREHENSIVE PROBLEM 1, Continued

ACCOUNT *Miscellaneous Expense* ACCOUNT NO. *59*

DATE		ITEM	POST. REF.	DEBIT	CREDIT	BALANCE	
						DEBIT	CREDIT

COMPREHENSIVE PROBLEM 1, Continued

3.

Unadjusted Trial Balance

Name ______________________

COMPREHENSIVE PROBLEM 1, Continued

5. Optional (Appendix)

	A	B	C	D	E	F	G	H	I	J	K
1											
2	End-of-Period Spreadsheet (Work Sheet)										
3											
4		Unadjusted				Adjusted		Income		Balance	
5		Trial Balance		Adjustments		Trial Balance		Statement		Sheet	
6	Account Title	Dr.	Cr.	Dr.	Cr.	Dr.	Cr.	Dr.	Cr.	Dr.	Cr.
7											
8											
9											
10											
11											
12											
13											
14											
15											
16											
17											
18											
19											
20											
21											
22											
23											
24											
25											
26											
27											
28											
29											
30											

Name ______________________________

COMPREHENSIVE PROBLEM 1, Continued

6.

JOURNAL

PAGE 7

DATE		DESCRIPTION	POST. REF.	DEBIT	CREDIT
		Adjusting Entries			

COMPREHENSIVE PROBLEM 1, Continued

7.

Adjusted Trial Balance

COMPREHENSIVE PROBLEM 1, Continued

8.

Income Statement

Statement of Owner's Equity

Name ______________________

COMPREHENSIVE PROBLEM 1, Continued

Balance Sheet

COMPREHENSIVE PROBLEM 1, Continued

9.

JOURNAL

PAGE *8*

	DATE		DESCRIPTION	POST. REF.	DEBIT	CREDIT	
1			*Closing Entries*				1
2							2
3							3
4							4
5							5
6							6
7							7
8							8
9							9
10							10
11							11
12							12
13							13
14							14
15							15
16							16
17							17
18							18
19							19
20							20
21							21
22							22
23							23
24							24
25							25
26							26
27							27
28							28
29							29
30							30
31							31
32							32
33							33
34							34
35							35

COMPREHENSIVE PROBLEM 1, Concluded

10.

Post-Closing Trial Balance

EXERCISE 5-1

REVENUE JOURNAL

Date	Invoice No.	Account Debited	Post. Ref.	Accounts Rec. Dr. Fees Earned Cr.
2016				
Mar. 1	112	Hazmat Safety Co.	(a) ________	$2,875
10	113	Masco Co.	(b) ________	980
20	114	Eco-Systems	(c) ________	1,700
27	115	Sunrise Enterprises	(d) ________	1,240
30				$6,795
				(e) ________

EXERCISE 5-2

a., b., and c.

Accounts Receivable

Eco-Systems

Hazmat Safety Co.

Masco Co.

Sunrise Enterprises

EXERCISE 5-2, Concluded

d.

Account Receivable Customer Balances	

EXERCISE 5-3

a. Closing of drawing account at the end of the year: ______________________

b. Providing services for cash: ______________________

c. Sale of office supplies on account, at cost, to a neighboring business: ______________________

d. Receipt of cash from sale of office equipment: ______________________

e. Receipt of cash for rent: ______________________

f. Receipt of cash on account from a customer: ______________________

g. Providing services on account: ______________________

h. Investment of additional cash in the business by the owner: ______________________

i. Receipt of cash refund from overpayment of taxes: ______________________

j. Adjustment to record accrued salaries at the end of the year: ______________________

EXERCISE 5-4

a. Purchase of office supplies for cash: ______________________

b. Advance payment of a one-year fire insurance policy on the office: ______________________

c. Purchase of office equipment for cash: ______________________

d. Adjustment to prepaid insurance at the end of the month: ______________________

e. Adjustment to prepaid rent at the end of the month: ______________________

f. Adjustment to record accrued salaries at the end of the period: ______________________

g. Purchase of services on account: ______________________

h. Purchase of office supplies on account: ______________________

i. Adjustment to record depreciation at the end of the month: ______________________

j. Payment of six months' rent in advance: ______________________

k. Purchase of an office computer on account: ______________________

EXERCISE 5-5

Apr. 3 ____

____

____

____

____

Apr. 6 ____

____

____

____

____

Apr. 24 ____

____

____

____

____

EXERCISE 5-6

a.

REVENUE JOURNAL PAGE

	DATE		INVOICE NO.	ACCOUNT DEBITED	POST. REF.	ACCTS. REC. DR. FEES EARNED CR.	
1							1
2							2
3							3
4							4
5							5
6							6
7							7
8							8
9							9
10							10

b. ____

____

____

c. ____

EXERCISE 5-7

a. and b.

Aladdin Co.

Clearmark Co.

Life Star Inc.

c.

Accounts Receivable

Fees Earned

EXERCISE 5-7, Concluded

d.

Accounts Receivable Customer Balances

e.

EXERCISE 5-8

Accounts Receivable Customer Balances

EXERCISE 5-8, Concluded

Accounts Receivable
(Controlling)

EXERCISE 5-9

REVENUE JOURNAL

PAGE *8*

	DATE		INVOICE NO.	ACCOUNT DEBITED	POST. REF.	ACCTS. REC. DR. FEES EARNED CR.	
1							1
2							2
3							3
4							4
5							5
6							6
7							7
8							8
9							9
10							10

CASH RECEIPTS JOURNAL

PAGE *12*

	DATE		ACCOUNT CREDITED	POST. REF.	FEES EARNED CR.	ACCOUNTS REC. CR.	CASH DR.	
1								1
2								2
3								3
4								4
5								5
6								6
7								7
8								8
9								9
10								10

EXERCISE 5-10

a.

REVENUE JOURNAL

PAGE 19

	DATE		INVOICE NO.	ACCOUNT DEBITED	POST. REF.	ACCTS. REC. DR. FEES EARNED CR.	
1							1
2							2
3							3
4							4
5							5
6							6
7							7
8							8
9							9
10							10

CASH RECEIPTS JOURNAL

PAGE 25

	DATE		ACCOUNT CREDITED	POST. REF.	FEES EARNED CR.	ACCOUNTS REC. CR.	CASH DR.	
1								1
2								2
3								3
4								4
5								5
6								6
7								7
8								8
9								9
10								10

EXERCISE 5-10, Concluded

b.

Accounts Receivable Customer Balances

Accounts Receivable

c. ______________________________

EXERCISE 5-11

a. ______
b. ______
c. ______
d. ______
e. ______
f. ______
g. ______
h. ______
i. ______
j. ______
k. ______
l. ______
m. ______

EXERCISE 5-12

a. ______
b. ______
c. ______
d. ______
e. ______
f. ______
g. ______
h. ______
i. ______
j. ______
k. ______
l. ______

EXERCISE 5-13

May 6 ______________________________

____

____

____

May 11 ______________________________

____

____

____

May 16 ______________________________

____

____

____

EXERCISE 5-14

a.

PURCHASES JOURNAL

	DATE		ACCOUNT CREDITED	POST. REF.	ACCOUNTS PAYABLE CR.	OFFICE SUPPLIES DR.	OTHER ACCOUNTS DR.			
							ACCOUNT	POST. REF.	AMOUNT	
1										1
2										2
3										3
4										4
5										5
6										6
7										7
8										8
9										9

b. ____

____

____

c. ____

Name ________________________________

EXERCISE 5-15

a. and b.

Enviro-Wash Supplies Inc.

Nicely Co.

Office Mate Inc.

c.

Accounts Payable

Cleaning Supplies

EXERCISE 5-15, Concluded

d.

Accounts Payable Creditor Balances

e.

Name ______________________________

EXERCISE 5-16

Accounts Payable Creditor Balances

Accounts Payable
(Controlling)

Name ______________________

EXERCISE 5-17

PURCHASES JOURNAL

PAGE 36

	DATE		ACCOUNT CREDITED	POST. REF.	ACCOUNTS PAYABLE CR.	CLEANING SUPPLIES DR.	OTHER ACCOUNTS DR. ACCOUNT	OTHER ACCOUNTS DR. POST. REF.	OTHER ACCOUNTS DR. AMOUNT	
1										1
2										2
3										3
4										4
5										5
6										6
7										7
8										8
9										9

CASH PAYMENTS JOURNAL

PAGE 41

	DATE		CK. NO.	ACCOUNT DEBITED	POST. REF.	OTHER ACCOUNTS DR.	ACCOUNTS PAYABLE DR.	CASH CR.	
1									1
2									2
3									3
4									4
5									5
6									6
7									7
8									8

Name ______________________

EXERCISE 5-18

a.

PURCHASES JOURNAL

PAGE 16

	DATE		ACCOUNT CREDITED	POST. REF.	ACCOUNTS PAYABLE CR.	PET SUPPLIES DR.	OTHER ACCOUNTS DR. ACCOUNT	OTHER ACCOUNTS DR. POST. REF.	OTHER ACCOUNTS DR. AMOUNT	
1										1
2										2
3										3
4										4
5										5
6										6
7										7
8										8

CASH PAYMENTS JOURNAL

PAGE 22

	DATE		CK. NO.	ACCOUNT DEBITED	POST. REF.	OTHER ACCOUNTS DR.	ACCOUNTS PAYABLE DR.	CASH CR.	
1									1
2									2
3									3
4									4
5									5
6									6
7									7
8									8

EXERCISE 5-18, Concluded

b.

Accounts Payable Creditor Balances

Accounts Payable

c.

EXERCISE 5-19

a.

b.

Accounts Payable Creditor Balances

EXERCISE 5-20

a.

b.

c.

d.

e.

EXERCISE 5-21

EXERCISE 5-22

a.

b.

EXERCISE 5-22, Concluded

c.

EXERCISE 5-23

a.

b.

JOURNAL PAGE 1

	DATE		DESCRIPTION	POST. REF.	DEBIT	CREDIT	
1							1
2							2
3							3
4							4

EXERCISE 5-23, Concluded

c. ______________________

d. ______________________

e. ______________________

EXERCISE 5-24

a. Amazon.com: ______________________

b. Dell Inc.: ______________________

c. DuPont: ______________________

d. Intuit Inc.: ______________________

e. L.L. Bean, Inc.: ______________________

f. W.W. Grainger, Inc.: ______________________

EXERCISE 5-25

a.

	RECENT YEAR (IN MILLIONS)	PRIOR YEAR (IN MILLIONS)	INCREASE (DECREASE)	
			AMOUNT	PERCENT

b.

	RECENT YEAR		PRIOR YEAR	
	AMOUNT	PERCENT	AMOUNT	PERCENT

EXERCISE 5-25, Concluded

c.

EXERCISE 5-26

a.

MAJOR PRODUCT SEGMENTS	FOR A RECENT YEAR (IN MILLIONS)	PERCENT

b.

EXERCISE 5-27

a.

	YEAR 2 (IN MILLIONS)	YEAR 1 (IN MILLIONS)	INCREASE (DECREASE)	
			AMOUNT	PERCENT

EXERCISE 5-27, Concluded

b.

	YEAR 2		YEAR 1	
	AMOUNT (IN MILLIONS)	PERCENT	AMOUNT (IN MILLIONS)	PERCENT

c.

PROBLEM 5-1 ___

1. and 2.

REVENUE JOURNAL

PAGE 1

	DATE		INVOICE NO.	ACCOUNT DEBITED	POST. REF.	ACCTS. REC. DR. FEES EARNED CR.	
1							1
2							2
3							3
4							4
5							5
6							6
7							7
8							8
9							9
10							10
11							11

JOURNAL

PAGE 1

	DATE		DESCRIPTION	POST. REF.	DEBIT	CREDIT	
1							1
2							2
3							3
4							4
5							5
6							6

PROBLEM 5-1 ___, Continued

ACCOUNTS RECEIVABLE SUBSIDIARY LEDGER

NAME

DATE	ITEM	POST. REF.	DEBIT	CREDIT	BALANCE

NAME

DATE	ITEM	POST. REF.	DEBIT	CREDIT	BALANCE

NAME

DATE	ITEM	POST. REF.	DEBIT	CREDIT	BALANCE

NAME

DATE	ITEM	POST. REF.	DEBIT	CREDIT	BALANCE

NAME

DATE	ITEM	POST. REF.	DEBIT	CREDIT	BALANCE

PROBLEM 5-1 ___, Concluded

2.

GENERAL LEDGER

ACCOUNT ACCOUNT NO.

DATE		ITEM	POST. REF.	DEBIT	CREDIT	BALANCE DEBIT	BALANCE CREDIT

ACCOUNT ACCOUNT NO.

DATE		ITEM	POST. REF.	DEBIT	CREDIT	BALANCE DEBIT	BALANCE CREDIT

ACCOUNT ACCOUNT NO.

DATE		ITEM	POST. REF.	DEBIT	CREDIT	BALANCE DEBIT	BALANCE CREDIT

3. a. ______________________________

b. ______________________________

4. ______________________________

This Page Not Used.

PROBLEM 5-2 ___

1. and 5.

GENERAL LEDGER

ACCOUNT ACCOUNT NO.

DATE		ITEM	POST. REF.	DEBIT	CREDIT	BALANCE	
						DEBIT	CREDIT

ACCOUNT ACCOUNT NO.

DATE		ITEM	POST. REF.	DEBIT	CREDIT	BALANCE	
						DEBIT	CREDIT

ACCOUNT ACCOUNT NO.

DATE		ITEM	POST. REF.	DEBIT	CREDIT	BALANCE	
						DEBIT	CREDIT

ACCOUNT ACCOUNT NO.

DATE		ITEM	POST. REF.	DEBIT	CREDIT	BALANCE	
						DEBIT	CREDIT

PROBLEM 5-2 ___, Continued

2. and 4.

ACCOUNTS RECEIVABLE SUBSIDIARY LEDGER

NAME

DATE		ITEM	POST. REF.	DEBIT	CREDIT	BALANCE

NAME

DATE		ITEM	POST. REF.	DEBIT	CREDIT	BALANCE

NAME

DATE		ITEM	POST. REF.	DEBIT	CREDIT	BALANCE

NAME

DATE		ITEM	POST. REF.	DEBIT	CREDIT	BALANCE

PROBLEM 5-2 ___, Continued

3., 4., and 5.

REVENUE JOURNAL

PAGE 40

	DATE		INVOICE NO.	ACCOUNT DEBITED	POST. REF.	ACCTS. REC. DR. FEES EARNED CR.	
1							1
2							2
3							3
4							4
5							5
6							6
7							7
8							8
9							9
10							10

CASH RECEIPTS JOURNAL

PAGE 36

	DATE		ACCOUNT CREDITED	POST. REF.	FEES EARNED CR.	ACCOUNTS REC. CR.	CASH DR.	
1								1
2								2
3								3
4								4
5								5
6								6
7								7
8								8
9								9
10								10

JOURNAL

PAGE 1

	DATE		DESCRIPTION	POST. REF.	DEBIT	CREDIT	
1							1
2							2
3							3
4							4
5							5

PROBLEM 5-2 ___, Concluded

6. ______________________________

7. ______________________________

PROBLEM 5-3 ___

1. and 4.

GENERAL LEDGER

ACCOUNT *Field Supplies* ACCOUNT NO. *14*

DATE		ITEM	POST. REF.	DEBIT	CREDIT	BALANCE DEBIT	BALANCE CREDIT

ACCOUNT *Office Supplies* ACCOUNT NO. *15*

DATE		ITEM	POST. REF.	DEBIT	CREDIT	BALANCE DEBIT	BALANCE CREDIT

ACCOUNT *Office Equipment* ACCOUNT NO. *18*

DATE		ITEM	POST. REF.	DEBIT	CREDIT	BALANCE DEBIT	BALANCE CREDIT

ACCOUNT *Accounts Payable* ACCOUNT NO. *21*

DATE		ITEM	POST. REF.	DEBIT	CREDIT	BALANCE DEBIT	BALANCE CREDIT

PROBLEM 5-3 ___, Continued

2. and 3.

ACCOUNTS PAYABLE SUBSIDIARY LEDGER

NAME

DATE		ITEM	POST. REF.	DEBIT	CREDIT	BALANCE

NAME

DATE		ITEM	POST. REF.	DEBIT	CREDIT	BALANCE

NAME

DATE		ITEM	POST. REF.	DEBIT	CREDIT	BALANCE

NAME

DATE		ITEM	POST. REF.	DEBIT	CREDIT	BALANCE

PROBLEM 5-3 ___, Continued

NAME

DATE		ITEM	POST. REF.	DEBIT	CREDIT	BALANCE

Name ______________________

PROBLEM 5-3 ___, Concluded

3. and 4.

PURCHASES JOURNAL

PAGE *30*

	DATE		ACCOUNT CREDITED	POST. REF.	ACCOUNTS PAYABLE CR.	FIELD SUPPLIES DR.	OFFICE SUPPLIES DR.	OTHER ACCOUNTS DR.			
								ACCOUNT	POST. REF.	AMOUNT	
1											1
2											2
3											3
4											4
5											5
6											6
7											7
8											8
9											9
10											10
11											11
12											12
13											13
14											14
15											15

5. a. ______________________

b. ______________________

6. ______________________

____

PROBLEM 5-4 ___

1., 2., and 3.

PURCHASES JOURNAL

PAGE *1*

	DATE		ACCOUNT CREDITED	POST. REF.	ACCOUNTS PAYABLE CR.	FIELD SUPPLIES DR.	OFFICE SUPPLIES DR.	OTHER ACCOUNTS DR.			
								ACCOUNT	POST. REF.	AMOUNT	
1											1
2											2
3											3
4											4
5											5
6											6
7											7
8											8
9											9
10											10
11											11
12											12
13											13
14											14
15											15
16											16
17											17
18											18
19											19
20											20

PROBLEM 5-4 ___, Continued

CASH PAYMENTS JOURNAL

PAGE 1

	DATE		CK. NO.	ACCOUNT DEBITED	POST. REF.	OTHER ACCOUNTS DR.	ACCOUNTS PAYABLE DR.	CASH CR.	
1									1
2									2
3									3
4									4
5									5
6									6
7									7
8									8
9									9
10									10
11									11
12									12
13									13
14									14
15									15

1. and 2.

JOURNAL

PAGE 1

	DATE		DESCRIPTION	POST. REF.	DEBIT	CREDIT	
1							1
2							2
3							3
4							4
5							5

PROBLEM 5-4 ___, Continued

1.

ACCOUNTS PAYABLE SUBSIDIARY LEDGER

NAME

DATE		ITEM	POST. REF.	DEBIT	CREDIT	BALANCE

NAME

DATE		ITEM	POST. REF.	DEBIT	CREDIT	BALANCE

NAME

DATE		ITEM	POST. REF.	DEBIT	CREDIT	BALANCE

PROBLEM 5-4 ___, Continued

2. and 3.

GENERAL LEDGER

ACCOUNT ACCOUNT NO.

DATE		ITEM	POST. REF.	DEBIT	CREDIT	BALANCE DEBIT	BALANCE CREDIT

ACCOUNT ACCOUNT NO.

DATE		ITEM	POST. REF.	DEBIT	CREDIT	BALANCE DEBIT	BALANCE CREDIT

ACCOUNT ACCOUNT NO.

DATE		ITEM	POST. REF.	DEBIT	CREDIT	BALANCE DEBIT	BALANCE CREDIT

ACCOUNT ACCOUNT NO.

DATE		ITEM	POST. REF.	DEBIT	CREDIT	BALANCE DEBIT	BALANCE CREDIT

ACCOUNT ACCOUNT NO.

DATE		ITEM	POST. REF.	DEBIT	CREDIT	BALANCE DEBIT	BALANCE CREDIT

PROBLEM 5-4 ___, Continued

ACCOUNT ACCOUNT NO.

DATE		ITEM	POST. REF.	DEBIT	CREDIT	BALANCE	
						DEBIT	CREDIT

ACCOUNT ACCOUNT NO.

DATE		ITEM	POST. REF.	DEBIT	CREDIT	BALANCE	
						DEBIT	CREDIT

ACCOUNT ACCOUNT NO.

DATE		ITEM	POST. REF.	DEBIT	CREDIT	BALANCE	
						DEBIT	CREDIT

ACCOUNT ACCOUNT NO.

DATE		ITEM	POST. REF.	DEBIT	CREDIT	BALANCE	
						DEBIT	CREDIT

ACCOUNT ACCOUNT NO.

DATE		ITEM	POST. REF.	DEBIT	CREDIT	BALANCE	
						DEBIT	CREDIT

PROBLEM 5-4 ___, Concluded

4.

Accounts Payable Creditor Balances

5. ____________________

PROBLEM 5-5 ___

1., 3., and 4.

GENERAL LEDGER

ACCOUNT *Cash* ACCOUNT NO. *11*

DATE		ITEM	POST. REF.	DEBIT	CREDIT	BALANCE	
						DEBIT	CREDIT

ACCOUNT *Accounts Receivable* ACCOUNT NO. *12*

DATE		ITEM	POST. REF.	DEBIT	CREDIT	BALANCE	
						DEBIT	CREDIT

ACCOUNT *Maintenance Supplies* ACCOUNT NO. *14*

DATE		ITEM	POST. REF.	DEBIT	CREDIT	BALANCE	
						DEBIT	CREDIT

ACCOUNT *Office Supplies* ACCOUNT NO. *15*

DATE		ITEM	POST. REF.	DEBIT	CREDIT	BALANCE	
						DEBIT	CREDIT

PROBLEM 5-5 ___, Continued

ACCOUNT *Office Equipment* ACCOUNT NO. *16*

DATE		ITEM	POST. REF.	DEBIT	CREDIT	BALANCE DEBIT	BALANCE CREDIT

ACCOUNT *Accumulated Depreciation—Office Equipment* ACCOUNT NO. *17*

DATE		ITEM	POST. REF.	DEBIT	CREDIT	BALANCE DEBIT	BALANCE CREDIT

ACCOUNT *Vehicles* ACCOUNT NO. *18*

DATE		ITEM	POST. REF.	DEBIT	CREDIT	BALANCE DEBIT	BALANCE CREDIT

ACCOUNT *Accumulated Depreciation—Vehicles* ACCOUNT NO. *19*

DATE		ITEM	POST. REF.	DEBIT	CREDIT	BALANCE DEBIT	BALANCE CREDIT

ACCOUNT *Accounts Payable* ACCOUNT NO. *21*

DATE		ITEM	POST. REF.	DEBIT	CREDIT	BALANCE DEBIT	BALANCE CREDIT

Name ______________________________

PROBLEM 5-5 ___, Continued

ACCOUNT ______________________, *Capital* ACCOUNT NO. *31*

DATE		ITEM	POST. REF.	DEBIT	CREDIT	BALANCE DEBIT	BALANCE CREDIT

ACCOUNT ______________________, *Drawing* ACCOUNT NO. *32*

DATE		ITEM	POST. REF.	DEBIT	CREDIT	BALANCE DEBIT	BALANCE CREDIT

ACCOUNT *Fees Earned* ACCOUNT NO. *41*

DATE		ITEM	POST. REF.	DEBIT	CREDIT	BALANCE DEBIT	BALANCE CREDIT

ACCOUNT *Rent Revenue* ACCOUNT NO. *42*

DATE		ITEM	POST. REF.	DEBIT	CREDIT	BALANCE DEBIT	BALANCE CREDIT

(This account is not used in Problem 5-5A.)

ACCOUNT *Driver Salaries Expense* ACCOUNT NO. *51*

DATE		ITEM	POST. REF.	DEBIT	CREDIT	BALANCE DEBIT	BALANCE CREDIT

PROBLEM 5-5 ___, Continued

ACCOUNT *Maintenance Supplies Expense* ACCOUNT NO. *52*

DATE		ITEM	POST. REF.	DEBIT	CREDIT	BALANCE	
						DEBIT	CREDIT

ACCOUNT *Fuel Expense* ACCOUNT NO. *53*

DATE		ITEM	POST. REF.	DEBIT	CREDIT	BALANCE	
						DEBIT	CREDIT

ACCOUNT *Office Salaries Expense* ACCOUNT NO. *61*

DATE		ITEM	POST. REF.	DEBIT	CREDIT	BALANCE	
						DEBIT	CREDIT

ACCOUNT *Rent Expense* ACCOUNT NO. *62*

DATE		ITEM	POST. REF.	DEBIT	CREDIT	BALANCE	
						DEBIT	CREDIT

ACCOUNT *Advertising Expense* ACCOUNT NO. *63*

DATE		ITEM	POST. REF.	DEBIT	CREDIT	BALANCE	
						DEBIT	CREDIT

ACCOUNT *Miscellaneous Administrative Expense* ACCOUNT NO. *64*

DATE		ITEM	POST. REF.	DEBIT	CREDIT	BALANCE	
						DEBIT	CREDIT

PROBLEM 5-5 ___, Continued

2. and 4.

PURCHASES JOURNAL

PAGE 37

	DATE		ACCOUNT CREDITED	POST. REF.	ACCOUNTS PAYABLE CR.	MAINTENANCE SUPPLIES DR.	OFFICE SUPPLIES DR.	OTHER ACCOUNTS DR.			
								ACCOUNT	POST. REF.	AMOUNT	
1											1
2											2
3											3
4											4
5											5
6											6
7											7
8											8
9											9
10											10
11											11
12											12
13											13
14											14
15											15
16											16
17											17
18											18
19											19
20											20

PROBLEM 5-5 ___, Continued

CASH RECEIPTS JOURNAL

PAGE *31*

	DATE		ACCOUNT CREDITED	POST. REF.	OTHER ACCOUNTS CR.	ACCOUNTS REC. CR.	CASH DR.	
1								1
2								2
3								3
4								4
5								5
6								6
7								7
8								8
9								9
10								10
11								11
12								12
13								13
14								14
15								15
16								16

REVENUE JOURNAL

PAGE *35*

	DATE		INVOICE NO.	ACCOUNT DEBITED	POST. REF.	ACCTS. REC. DR. FEES EARNED CR.	
1							1
2							2
3							3
4							4
5							5
6							6
7							7
8							8
9							9
10							10
11							11
12							12
13							13
14							14

Name ______________________________

PROBLEM 5-5 ___, Continued

CASH PAYMENTS JOURNAL

PAGE 34

	DATE		CK. NO.	ACCOUNT DEBITED	POST. REF.	OTHER ACCOUNTS DR.	ACCOUNTS PAYABLE DR.	CASH CR.	
1									1
2									2
3									3
4									4
5									5
6									6
7									7
8									8
9									9
10									10
11									11
12									12
13									13
14									14
15									15
16									16
17									17
18									18
19									19
20									20
21									21
22									22

3.

JOURNAL

PAGE 1

	DATE		DESCRIPTION	POST. REF.	DEBIT	CREDIT	
1							1
2							2
3							3
4							4
5							5

PROBLEM 5-5 ___, Concluded

5.

Unadjusted Trial Balance

Name ______________________________

EXERCISE 6-1

a. ______________________________

b. ______________________________

c. ______________________________

EXERCISE 6-2

EXERCISE 6-3

a. ______________________________

b. ______________________________

EXERCISE 6-4

EXERCISE 6-5

(1) ______________________

(2) ______________________

(3) ______________________

(4) ______________________

EXERCISE 6-6

JOURNAL

PAGE

	DATE		DESCRIPTION	POST. REF.	DEBIT	CREDIT	
1							1
2							2
3							3
4							4
5							5
6							6
7							7
8							8
9							9
10							10
11							11
12							12

EXERCISE 6-7

JOURNAL

PAGE

	DATE		DESCRIPTION	POST. REF.	DEBIT	CREDIT	
1							1
2							2
3							3
4							4
5							5
6							6
7							7
8							8
9							9
10							10
11							11
12							12
13							13
14							14
15							15
16							16
17							17
18							18
19							19
20							20
21							21
22							22
23							23
24							24

EXERCISE 6-8

JOURNAL

PAGE

DATE		DESCRIPTION	POST. REF.	DEBIT	CREDIT

EXERCISE 6-9

a and b.

JOURNAL PAGE

	DATE		DESCRIPTION	POST. REF.	DEBIT	CREDIT	
1							1
2							2
3							3
4							4
5							5
6							6
7							7
8							8
9							9
10							10
11							11
12							12
13							13
14							14
15							15
16							16
17							17
18							18

EXERCISE 6-10

a. ____

b.

JOURNAL PAGE

	DATE		DESCRIPTION	POST. REF.	DEBIT	CREDIT	
1							1
2							2
3							3
4							4
5							5
6							6
7							7
8							8

EXERCISE 6-11

(1) ______________________

____

____

(2) ______________________

____

____

(3) ______________________

____

____

(4) ______________________

____

____

(5) ______________________

____

____

EXERCISE 6-12

a. Amount of the sale: ______________________

b. Amount debited to Accounts Receivable: ______________________

c. Amount received within the discount period: ______________________

EXERCISE 6-13

	Merchandise	Freight Paid by Seller		Customer Returns and Allowances	Amount to be Paid in Full
a.	$27,000	—	FOB destination, n/30	$4,500	$__________
b.	18,600	$475	FOB shipping point, 2/10, n/30	3,000	$__________
c.	8,400	—	FOB shipping point, 1/10, n/30	700	$__________
d.	48,300	900	FOB shipping point, 2/10, n/30	6,500	$__________
e.	33,000	—	FOB destination, 1/10, n/30	—	$__________

Name ______________________________

EXERCISE 6-14

JOURNAL PAGE

	DATE		DESCRIPTION	POST. REF.	DEBIT	CREDIT	
1							1
2							2
3							3
4							4
5							5
6							6
7							7
8							8
9							9
10							10
11							11
12							12
13							13
14							14
15							15
16							16
17							17
18							18
19							19
20							20
21							21
22							22
23							23
24							24

EXERCISE 6-15

JOURNAL

PAGE

	DATE		DESCRIPTION	POST. REF.	DEBIT	CREDIT	
1							1
2							2
3							3
4							4
5							5
6							6
7							7
8							8
9							9
10							10
11							11
12							12
13							13
14							14

Name ______________________________

EXERCISE 6-16

Balance Sheet Accounts

Acct. #	Account Name

Income Statement Accounts

Acct. #	Account Name

EXERCISE 6-17

a. ______________________________

b. ______________________________

c. ______________________________

d. ______________________________

EXERCISE 6-18

JOURNAL PAGE

	DATE		DESCRIPTION	POST. REF.	DEBIT	CREDIT	
1							1
2							2
3							3
4							4
5							5
6							6
7							7
8							8
9							9
10							10
11							11
12							12

EXERCISE 6-19

	Debit	Credit
a. Cost of Merchandise Sold..........................	________	________
b. Customer Refunds Payable.......................	________	________
c. Delivery Expense..	________	________
d. Estimated Returns Inventory	________	________
e. Merchandise Inventory...............................	________	________
f. Sales..	________	________
g. Sales Tax Payable......................................	________	________

EXERCISE 6-20

a. Gross profit: ______________________________

b. ______________________________

____

c. ______________________________

____

d. ______________________________

____

EXERCISE 6-21

1. Advertising expense: ______________________________

2. Depreciation expense on store equipment: ______________________________

3. Insurance expense on office equipment: ______________________________

4. Interest expense on notes payable: ______________________________

5. Rent expense on office building: ______________________________

6. Salaries of office personnel: ______________________________

7. Salary of sales manager: ______________________________

8. Sales supplies used: ______________________________

EXERCISE 6-22

Sales	$463,400	**(b)** $________	$1,295,000	**(d)** $________
Cost of merchandise sold	**(a)** ________	410,000	**(c)** ________	900,000
Gross profit	83,500	277,500	275,000	600,000

EXERCISE 6-23

a.

Income Statement

b. ______________________

EXERCISE 6-24

(Optional)

Income Statement

EXERCISE 6-25

Income Statement

EXERCISE 6-26

JOURNAL PAGE

	DATE		DESCRIPTION	POST. REF.	DEBIT	CREDIT	
1							1
2							2
3							3
4							4
5							5

EXERCISE 6-27

a. Accounts Payable: ______________________

b. Advertising Expense: ______________________

c. Cost of Merchandise Sold: ______________________

d. Merchandise Inventory: ______________________

e. Sales: ______________________

f. Supplies: ______________________

g. Supplies Expense: ______________________

h. Valery Lavine, Drawing: ______________________

i. Wages Payable: ______________________

EXERCISE 6-28

JOURNAL PAGE

	DATE		DESCRIPTION	POST. REF.	DEBIT	CREDIT	
1			*Closing Entries*				1
2							2
3							3
4							4
5							5
6							6
7							7
8							8
9							9
10							10
11							11
12							12
13							13
14							14
15							15
16							16
17							17
18							18
19							19
20							20
21							21
22							22
23							23
24							24

EXERCISE 6-29

JOURNAL PAGE

	DATE		DESCRIPTION	POST. REF.	DEBIT	CREDIT	
1			*Closing Entries*				1
2							2
3							3
4							4
5							5
6							6
7							7
8							8
9							9
10							10
11							11
12							12
13							13
14							14
15							15
16							16
17							17
18							18
19							19
20							20
21							21
22							22
23							23
24							24

EXERCISE 6-30

a. Year 2: ______________________________

Year 1: ______________________________

b. ______________________________

____

____

____

____

____

EXERCISE 6-31

a. ____________________

b. ____________________

APPENDIX EXERCISE 6-32

Account	Increase	Decrease	Normal Balance
Purchases	debit	(a) ________	(b) ________
Purchase Discounts	credit	(c) ________	credit
Purchase Returns and Allowances	(d) ________	(e) ________	(f) ________
Freight In	debit	(g) ________	debit

APPENDIX EXERCISE 6-33

JOURNAL

PAGE

DATE		DESCRIPTION	POST. REF.	DEBIT	CREDIT

APPENDIX EXERCISE 6-34

a. Purchases – (X + Y) = Net purchases

____

b. Net purchases + X = Cost of merchandise purchased

____

c. Merchandise inventory (beginning) + Cost of merchandise purchased = X

____

d. Merchandise available for sale – X = Cost of merchandise sold

____

APPENDIX EXERCISE 6-35

a.

b. ______________________________

c. ______________________________

____

APPENDIX EXERCISE 6-36

APPENDIX EXERCISE 6-37

APPENDIX EXERCISE 6-38

(Optional)

Name ________________________________

APPENDIX EXERCISE 6-39

JOURNAL

PAGE

DATE		DESCRIPTION	POST. REF.	DEBIT	CREDIT
		Closing Entries			

This Page Not Used.

Name ______________________________

PROBLEM 6-1 ___

JOURNAL

PAGE

DATE		DESCRIPTION	POST. REF.	DEBIT	CREDIT

PROBLEM 6-1 ___, Concluded

JOURNAL

PAGE

	DATE		DESCRIPTION	POST. REF.	DEBIT	CREDIT	
1							1
2							2
3							3
4							4
5							5
6							6
7							7
8							8
9							9
10							10
11							11
12							12
13							13
14							14
15							15
16							16
17							17
18							18
19							19
20							20
21							21
22							22
23							23
24							24
25							25
26							26
27							27
28							28
29							29
30							30
31							31
32							32
33							33
34							34
35							35
36							36

PROBLEM 6-2 ___

JOURNAL

PAGE

	DATE		DESCRIPTION	POST. REF.	DEBIT	CREDIT	
1							1
2							2
3							3
4							4
5							5
6							6
7							7
8							8
9							9
10							10
11							11
12							12
13							13
14							14
15							15
16							16
17							17
18							18
19							19
20							20
21							21
22							22
23							23
24							24
25							25
26							26
27							27
28							28
29							29
30							30
31							31
32							32
33							33
34							34
35							35
36							36

PROBLEM 6-2 ___, Continued

JOURNAL

PAGE

	DATE		DESCRIPTION	POST. REF.	DEBIT	CREDIT	
1							1
2							2
3							3
4							4
5							5
6							6
7							7
8							8
9							9
10							10
11							11
12							12
13							13
14							14
15							15
16							16
17							17
18							18
19							19
20							20
21							21
22							22
23							23
24							24
25							25
26							26
27							27
28							28
29							29
30							30
31							31
32							32
33							33
34							34
35							35
36							36

PROBLEM 6-2 ___, Concluded

JOURNAL

PAGE

	DATE		DESCRIPTION	POST. REF.	DEBIT	CREDIT	
1							1
2							2
3							3
4							4
5							5
6							6
7							7
8							8
9							9
10							10
11							11
12							12
13							13
14							14
15							15
16							16
17							17
18							18
19							19
20							20
21							21
22							22
23							23
24							24
25							25
26							26
27							27
28							28
29							29
30							30
31							31
32							32
33							33
34							34
35							35
36							36

This Page Not Used.

Name ______________________

PROBLEM 6-3 ___

JOURNAL

PAGE

	DATE		DESCRIPTION	POST. REF.	DEBIT	CREDIT	
1							1
2							2
3							3
4							4
5							5
6							6
7							7
8							8
9							9
10							10
11							11
12							12
13							13
14							14
15							15
16							16
17							17
18							18
19							19
20							20
21							21
22							22
23							23
24							24
25							25
26							26
27							27
28							28
29							29
30							30
31							31
32							32
33							33
34							34
35							35
36							36

PROBLEM 6-3 ___, Concluded

JOURNAL

PAGE

	DATE		DESCRIPTION	POST. REF.	DEBIT	CREDIT	
1							1
2							2
3							3
4							4
5							5
6							6
7							7
8							8
9							9
10							10
11							11
12							12
13							13
14							14
15							15
16							16
17							17
18							18
19							19
20							20
21							21
22							22
23							23
24							24
25							25
26							26
27							27
28							28
29							29
30							30
31							31
32							32
33							33
34							34
35							35
36							36

PROBLEM 6-4 ___

1.

JOURNAL

PAGE

	DATE		DESCRIPTION	POST. REF.	DEBIT	CREDIT	
1							1
2							2
3							3
4							4
5							5
6							6
7							7
8							8
9							9
10							10
11							11
12							12
13							13
14							14
15							15
16							16
17							17
18							18
19							19
20							20
21							21
22							22
23							23
24							24
25							25
26							26
27							27
28							28
29							29
30							30
31							31
32							32
33							33
34							34
35							35

PROBLEM 6-4 ___, Continued

JOURNAL

PAGE

	DATE		DESCRIPTION	POST. REF.	DEBIT	CREDIT	
1							1
2							2
3							3
4							4
5							5
6							6
7							7
8							8
9							9
10							10
11							11
12							12
13							13
14							14
15							15
16							16
17							17
18							18
19							19
20							20
21							21
22							22
23							23
24							24
25							25
26							26
27							27
28							28
29							29
30							30
31							31
32							32
33							33
34							34
35							35
36							36

Name ______________________________

PROBLEM 6-4 ___, Concluded

2.

JOURNAL

PAGE

	DATE		DESCRIPTION	POST. REF.	DEBIT	CREDIT	
1							1
2							2
3							3
4							4
5							5
6							6
7							7
8							8
9							9
10							10
11							11
12							12
13							13
14							14
15							15
16							16
17							17
18							18
19							19
20							20
21							21
22							22
23							23
24							24
25							25
26							26
27							27
28							28
29							29
30							30
31							31
32							32
33							33
34							34
35							35

This Page Not Used.

PROBLEM 6-5 ___

1.

Income Statement

PROBLEM 6-5 ___, Continued

2.

Statement of Owner's Equity

Name ____________________

PROBLEM 6-5 ___, Continued

3.

Balance Sheet

PROBLEM 6-5 ___, Concluded

4. a.

b.

PROBLEM 6-6 ___

1.

Income Statement

2.

Statement of Owner's Equity

Name ______________________

PROBLEM 6-6 ___, Continued

3.

Balance Sheet

PROBLEM 6-6 ___, Concluded

4.

JOURNAL

PAGE

	DATE		DESCRIPTION	POST. REF.	DEBIT	CREDIT	
1			*Closing Entries*				1
2							2
3							3
4							4
5							5
6							6
7							7
8							8
9							9
10							10
11							11
12							12
13							13
14							14
15							15
16							16
17							17
18							18
19							19
20							20
21							21
22							22
23							23
24							24
25							25
26							26
27							27
28							28
29							29
30							30
31							31
32							32
33							33
34							34
35							35

This Page Not Used.

APPENDIX PROBLEM 6-7 ___

JOURNAL

PAGE

	DATE		DESCRIPTION	POST. REF.	DEBIT	CREDIT	
1							1
2							2
3							3
4							4
5							5
6							6
7							7
8							8
9							9
10							10
11							11
12							12
13							13
14							14
15							15
16							16
17							17
18							18
19							19
20							20
21							21
22							22
23							23
24							24
25							25
26							26
27							27
28							28
29							29
30							30
31							31
32							32
33							33
34							34
35							35
36							36

APPENDIX PROBLEM 6-7 ___, Concluded

JOURNAL

PAGE

DATE		DESCRIPTION	POST. REF.	DEBIT	CREDIT

APPENDIX PROBLEM 6-8 ___

JOURNAL

PAGE

	DATE		DESCRIPTION	POST. REF.	DEBIT	CREDIT	
1							1
2							2
3							3
4							4
5							5
6							6
7							7
8							8
9							9
10							10
11							11
12							12
13							13
14							14
15							15
16							16
17							17
18							18
19							19
20							20
21							21
22							22
23							23
24							24
25							25
26							26
27							27
28							28
29							29
30							30
31							31
32							32
33							33
34							34
35							35
36							36

APPENDIX PROBLEM 6-8 ___, Concluded

JOURNAL

PAGE

	DATE		DESCRIPTION	POST. REF.	DEBIT	CREDIT	
1							1
2							2
3							3
4							4
5							5
6							6
7							7
8							8
9							9
10							10
11							11
12							12
13							13
14							14
15							15
16							16
17							17
18							18
19							19
20							20
21							21
22							22
23							23
24							24
25							25
26							26
27							27
28							28
29							29
30							30
31							31
32							32
33							33
34							34
35							35
36							36

APPENDIX PROBLEM 6-9 ___

1.

JOURNAL

PAGE

	DATE		DESCRIPTION	POST. REF.	DEBIT	CREDIT	
1							1
2							2
3							3
4							4
5							5
6							6
7							7
8							8
9							9
10							10
11							11
12							12
13							13
14							14
15							15
16							16
17							17
18							18
19							19
20							20
21							21
22							22
23							23
24							24
25							25
26							26
27							27
28							28
29							29
30							30
31							31
32							32
33							33
34							34
35							35

APPENDIX PROBLEM 6-9 ___, Concluded

2.

JOURNAL PAGE

	DATE		DESCRIPTION	POST. REF.	DEBIT	CREDIT	
1							1
2							2
3							3
4							4
5							5
6							6
7							7
8							8
9							9
10							10
11							11
12							12
13							13
14							14
15							15
16							16
17							17
18							18
19							19
20							20
21							21
22							22
23							23
24							24
25							25
26							26
27							27
28							28
29							29
30							30
31							31
32							32
33							33
34							34
35							35

APPENDIX PROBLEM 6-10 ___

1. ______________________________

2.

Income Statement

APPENDIX PROBLEM 6-10 ___, Continued

Income Statement (Continued)

APPENDIX PROBLEM 6-10 ___, Continued

3.

JOURNAL

PAGE

DATE		DESCRIPTION	POST. REF.	DEBIT	CREDIT
		Closing Entries			

APPENDIX PROBLEM 6-10 ___, Concluded

JOURNAL

PAGE

	DATE		DESCRIPTION	POST. REF.	DEBIT	CREDIT	
1			*Closing Entries*				1
2							2
3							3
4							4
5							5
6							6
7							7
8							8
9							9
10							10
11							11
12							12
13							13
14							14
15							15
16							16
17							17
18							18
19							19
20							20
21							21
22							22
23							23
24							24
25							25
26							26
27							27
28							28
29							29
30							30
31							31
32							32

4. ____

____

COMPREHENSIVE PROBLEM 2

1., 2., 6., and 9.

GENERAL LEDGER

ACCOUNT *Cash* ACCOUNT NO. *110*

DATE		ITEM	POST. REF.	DEBIT	CREDIT	BALANCE	
						DEBIT	CREDIT

ACCOUNT *Accounts Receivable* ACCOUNT NO. *112*

DATE		ITEM	POST. REF.	DEBIT	CREDIT	BALANCE	
						DEBIT	CREDIT

COMPREHENSIVE PROBLEM 2, Continued

ACCOUNT *Merchandise Inventory* ACCOUNT NO. *115*

DATE		ITEM	POST. REF.	DEBIT	CREDIT	BALANCE	
						DEBIT	CREDIT

ACCOUNT *Estimated Returns Inventory* ACCOUNT NO. *116*

DATE		ITEM	POST. REF.	DEBIT	CREDIT	BALANCE	
						DEBIT	CREDIT

ACCOUNT *Prepaid Insurance* ACCOUNT NO. *117*

DATE		ITEM	POST. REF.	DEBIT	CREDIT	BALANCE	
						DEBIT	CREDIT

COMPREHENSIVE PROBLEM 2, Continued

ACCOUNT *Store Supplies* ACCOUNT NO. *118*

DATE	ITEM	POST. REF.	DEBIT	CREDIT	BALANCE	
					DEBIT	CREDIT

ACCOUNT *Store Equipment* ACCOUNT NO. *123*

DATE	ITEM	POST. REF.	DEBIT	CREDIT	BALANCE	
					DEBIT	CREDIT

ACCOUNT *Accumulated Depreciation—Store Equipment* ACCOUNT NO. *124*

DATE	ITEM	POST. REF.	DEBIT	CREDIT	BALANCE	
					DEBIT	CREDIT

ACCOUNT *Accounts Payable* ACCOUNT NO. *210*

DATE	ITEM	POST. REF.	DEBIT	CREDIT	BALANCE	
					DEBIT	CREDIT

COMPREHENSIVE PROBLEM 2, Continued

ACCOUNT *Salaries Payable* ACCOUNT NO. *211*

DATE		ITEM	POST. REF.	DEBIT	CREDIT	BALANCE DEBIT	BALANCE CREDIT

ACCOUNT *Customer Refunds Payable* ACCOUNT NO. *212*

DATE		ITEM	POST. REF.	DEBIT	CREDIT	BALANCE DEBIT	BALANCE CREDIT

ACCOUNT *Lynn Tolley, Capital* ACCOUNT NO. *310*

DATE		ITEM	POST. REF.	DEBIT	CREDIT	BALANCE DEBIT	BALANCE CREDIT

ACCOUNT *Lynn Tolley, Drawing* ACCOUNT NO. *311*

DATE		ITEM	POST. REF.	DEBIT	CREDIT	BALANCE DEBIT	BALANCE CREDIT

Name ______________________

COMPREHENSIVE PROBLEM 2, Continued

ACCOUNT *Income Summary* ACCOUNT NO. *312*

DATE		ITEM	POST. REF.	DEBIT	CREDIT	BALANCE DEBIT	BALANCE CREDIT

ACCOUNT *Sales* ACCOUNT NO. *410*

DATE		ITEM	POST. REF.	DEBIT	CREDIT	BALANCE DEBIT	BALANCE CREDIT

ACCOUNT *Cost of Merchandise Sold* ACCOUNT NO. *510*

DATE		ITEM	POST. REF.	DEBIT	CREDIT	BALANCE DEBIT	BALANCE CREDIT

COMPREHENSIVE PROBLEM 2, Continued

ACCOUNT *Sales Salaries Expense* ACCOUNT NO. *520*

DATE		ITEM	POST. REF.	DEBIT	CREDIT	BALANCE	
						DEBIT	CREDIT

ACCOUNT *Advertising Expense* ACCOUNT NO. *521*

DATE		ITEM	POST. REF.	DEBIT	CREDIT	BALANCE	
						DEBIT	CREDIT

ACCOUNT *Depreciation Expense* ACCOUNT NO. *522*

DATE		ITEM	POST. REF.	DEBIT	CREDIT	BALANCE	
						DEBIT	CREDIT

ACCOUNT *Store Supplies Expense* ACCOUNT NO. *523*

DATE		ITEM	POST. REF.	DEBIT	CREDIT	BALANCE	
						DEBIT	CREDIT

COMPREHENSIVE PROBLEM 2, Continued

ACCOUNT *Miscellaneous Selling Expense* ACCOUNT NO. 529

DATE		ITEM	POST. REF.	DEBIT	CREDIT	BALANCE	
						DEBIT	CREDIT

ACCOUNT *Office Salaries Expense* ACCOUNT NO. 530

DATE		ITEM	POST. REF.	DEBIT	CREDIT	BALANCE	
						DEBIT	CREDIT

ACCOUNT *Rent Expense* ACCOUNT NO. 531

DATE		ITEM	POST. REF.	DEBIT	CREDIT	BALANCE	
						DEBIT	CREDIT

ACCOUNT *Insurance Expense* ACCOUNT NO. 532

DATE		ITEM	POST. REF.	DEBIT	CREDIT	BALANCE	
						DEBIT	CREDIT

COMPREHENSIVE PROBLEM 2, Continued

ACCOUNT *Miscellaneous Administrative Expense* ACCOUNT NO. *539*

DATE		ITEM	POST. REF.	DEBIT	CREDIT	BALANCE	
						DEBIT	CREDIT

Name ______________________________

COMPREHENSIVE PROBLEM 2, Continued

1. and 2.

JOURNAL

PAGE *20*

DATE		DESCRIPTION	POST. REF.	DEBIT	CREDIT

COMPREHENSIVE PROBLEM 2, Continued

JOURNAL

PAGE *20*
continued

	DATE		DESCRIPTION	POST. REF.	DEBIT	CREDIT	
1							1
2							2
3							3
4							4
5							5
6							6
7							7
8							8
9							9
10							10
11							11
12							12
13							13
14							14
15							15
16							16
17							17
18							18
19							19
20							20
21							21
22							22
23							23
24							24
25							25
26							26
27							27
28							28
29							29
30							30
31							31
32							32
33							33
34							34
35							35

COMPREHENSIVE PROBLEM 2, Continued

JOURNAL

PAGE *21*

DATE		DESCRIPTION	POST. REF.	DEBIT	CREDIT

COMPREHENSIVE PROBLEM 2, Continued

JOURNAL

PAGE *21*
continued

	DATE		DESCRIPTION	POST. REF.	DEBIT	CREDIT	
1							1
2							2
3							3
4							4
5							5
6							6
7							7
8							8
9							9
10							10
11							11
12							12
13							13
14							14
15							15
16							16
17							17
18							18
19							19
20							20
21							21
22							22
23							23
24							24
25							25
26							26
27							27
28							28
29							29
30							30
31							31
32							32
33							33
34							34
35							35

Name ______________________________

COMPREHENSIVE PROBLEM 2, Continued

3.

Unadjusted Trial Balance

COMPREHENSIVE PROBLEM 2, Continued

4. and 6.

JOURNAL

PAGE *22*

DATE		DESCRIPTION	POST. REF.	DEBIT	CREDIT
		Adjusting Entries			

COMPREHENSIVE PROBLEM 2, Continued

7.

Adjusted Trial Balance

COMPREHENSIVE PROBLEM 2, Continued

8.

Income Statement

COMPREHENSIVE PROBLEM 2, Continued

Statement of Owner's Equity

COMPREHENSIVE PROBLEM 2, Continued

Balance Sheet

COMPREHENSIVE PROBLEM 2, Continued

9.

JOURNAL

PAGE *23*

DATE		DESCRIPTION	POST. REF.	DEBIT	CREDIT
		Closing Entries			

COMPREHENSIVE PROBLEM 2, Continued

10.

Post-Closing Trial Balance

COMPREHENSIVE PROBLEM 2, Concluded

5. **(Optional)** *This work sheet is applicable only if the end-of-period spreadsheet (work sheet) is used.*

	A	B	C	D	E	F	G	H	I	J	K
1											
2	End-of-Period Spreadsheet (Work Sheet)										
3											
4		Unadjusted Trial Balance		Adjustments		Adjusted Trial Balance		Income Statement		Balance Sheet	
5											
6	Account Title	Dr.	Cr.	Dr.	Cr.	Dr.	Cr.	Dr.	Cr.	Dr.	Cr.
7											
8											
9											
10											
11											
12											
13											
14											
15											
16											
17											
18											
19											
20											
21											
22											
23											
24											
25											
26											
27											
28											
29											
30											
31											
32											
33											

This Page Not Used.

EXERCISE 7-1

EXERCISE 7-2

a.

b.

c.

Name ______________________

EXERCISE 7-3

a.

Portable DVD Players									
Date	Purchases			Cost of Merchandise Sold			Inventory		
	Quantity	Unit Cost	Total Cost	Quantity	Unit Cost	Total Cost	Quantity	Unit Cost	Total Cost

b. ____

____

____

EXERCISE 7-4

Portable DVD Players									
Date	Purchases			Cost of Merchandise Sold			Inventory		
	Quantity	Unit Cost	Total Cost	Quantity	Unit Cost	Total Cost	Quantity	Unit Cost	Total Cost

Name ______________________

EXERCISE 7-5

a.

Prepaid Cell Phones									
Date	Purchases			Cost of Merchandise Sold			Inventory		
	Quantity	Unit Cost	Total Cost	Quantity	Unit Cost	Total Cost	Quantity	Unit Cost	Total Cost

b. ______________________

____

____

EXERCISE 7-6

Prepaid Cell Phones									
Date	Purchases			Cost of Merchandise Sold			Inventory		
	Quantity	Unit Cost	Total Cost	Quantity	Unit Cost	Total Cost	Quantity	Unit Cost	Total Cost

EXERCISE 7-7

a. FIFO: ____________________

____

b. LIFO: ____________________

____

EXERCISE 7-8

Date	Purchases			Cost of Merchandise Sold			Inventory		
	Quantity	Unit Cost	Total Cost	Quantity	Unit Cost	Total Cost	Quantity	Unit Cost	Total Cost

Name ______________________________

EXERCISE 7-9

Date	Purchases			Cost of Merchandise Sold			Inventory		
	Quantity	Unit Cost	Total Cost	Quantity	Unit Cost	Total Cost	Quantity	Unit Cost	Total Cost

EXERCISE 7-10

Date	Purchases			Cost of Merchandise Sold			Inventory		
	Quantity	Unit Cost	Total Cost	Quantity	Unit Cost	Total Cost	Quantity	Unit Cost	Total Cost

EXERCISE 7-11

Date	Purchases			Cost of Merchandise Sold			Inventory		
	Quantity	Unit Cost	Total Cost	Quantity	Unit Cost	Total Cost	Quantity	Unit Cost	Total Cost

EXERCISE 7-12

a. First-in, first-out method: ____

____

b. Last-in, first-out method: ____

____

c. Weighted average cost method: ______________________________________

____

____

____

____

____

____

____

EXERCISE 7-13

	Cost	
Inventory Method	**Merchandise Inventory**	**Merchandise Sold**
a. First-in, first-out	________	________
b. Last-in, first-out	________	________
c. Weighted average cost	________	________

Supporting calculations:

EXERCISE 7-14

a. 1. FIFO inventory _________ LIFO inventory

2. FIFO cost of goods sold _________ LIFO cost of goods sold

3. FIFO net income _________ LIFO net income

4. FIFO income taxes _________ LIFO income taxes

b. ______________________________

____

____

____

____

EXERCISE 7-15

	A	B	C	D	E	F	G
1				Market	Total		
2				Value			
3	Commodity	Inventory Quantity	Cost per Unit	per Unit (Net Realizable Value)	Cost	Market	LCM
4	Ash	80	$140	$125			
5	Aspen	120	90	112			
6	Beech	30	75	74			
7	Maple	75	88	86			
8	Oak	60	140	145			
9	Total						

EXERCISE 7-16

____

____

____

____

____

____

____

EXERCISE 7-17

a.

Balance Sheet

Merchandise inventory	______
Current assets	______
Total assets	______
Owner's equity	______

b.

Income Statement

Cost of merchandise sold	______
Gross profit	______
Net income	______

c.

Income Statement

Cost of merchandise sold	______
Gross profit	______
Net income	______

d. ______

EXERCISE 7-18

a.

	Balance Sheet
Merchandise inventory	______________
Current assets	______________
Total assets	______________
Owner's equity	______________

b.

	Income Statement
Cost of merchandise sold	______________
Gross profit	______________
Net income	______________

c.

	Income Statement
Cost of merchandise sold	______________
Gross profit	______________
Net income	______________

d. ____

____

____

____

EXERCISE 7-19

EXERCISE 7-20

a. Apple: ______________________

American Greetings: ______________________

b. ______________________

EXERCISE 7-21

a. Number of Days' Sales in Inventory =

____

Kroger: ____

____

Safeway: _______________________________________

____

Whole Foods: ___________________________________

____

Inventory Turnover =

____

Kroger: ____

____

Safeway: _______________________________________

____

Whole Foods: ___________________________________

____

b. ____

____

____

____

____

____

____

____

____

____

EXERCISE 7-21, Concluded

c.

APPENDIX EXERCISE 7-22

APPENDIX EXERCISE 7-23

APPENDIX EXERCISE 7-24

APPENDIX EXERCISE 7-25

	A	B	C
1		Cost	Retail
2			
3			
4			
5			
6			
7			
8			
9			
10			

APPENDIX EXERCISE 7-26

a.

	A	B	C
1			
2			
3			
4			
5			
6			
7			
8			
9			
10			

b. ____________________

APPENDIX EXERCISE 7-27

APPENDIX EXERCISE 7-28

Name ____________________

PROBLEM 7-1 ___

1.

Date	Purchases			Cost of Merchandise Sold			Inventory		
	Quantity	Unit Cost	Total Cost	Quantity	Unit Cost	Total Cost	Quantity	Unit Cost	Total Cost

PROBLEM 7-1 ___, Concluded

2.

JOURNAL

PAGE

	DATE		DESCRIPTION	POST. REF.	DEBIT	CREDIT	
1							1
2							2
3							3
4							4
5							5
6							6
7							7
8							8
9							9
10							10

3. ______________________________

4. ______________________________

5. ______________________________

Name ____________________

PROBLEM 7-2 ___

1.

Date	Purchases			Cost of Merchandise Sold			Inventory		
	Quantity	Unit Cost	Total Cost	Quantity	Unit Cost	Total Cost	Quantity	Unit Cost	Total Cost

Name ______________________

PROBLEM 7-2 ___, Continued

Date	Purchases			Cost of Merchandise Sold			Inventory		
	Quantity	Unit Cost	Total Cost	Quantity	Unit Cost	Total Cost	Quantity	Unit Cost	Total Cost

PROBLEM 7-2 ___, Concluded

2.

3. ____

____

This Page Not Used.

PROBLEM 7-3 ___

Date	Purchases			Cost of Merchandise Sold			Inventory		
	Quantity	Unit Cost	Total Cost	Quantity	Unit Cost	Total Cost	Quantity	Unit Cost	Total Cost

PROBLEM 7-3 ___, Concluded

2.

3. ____

____

PROBLEM 7-4 ___

1., 2., and 3.

	Cost	
Inventory Method	**Merchandise Inventory**	**Merchandise Sold**
a. First-in, first-out................................	______	______
b. Last-in, first-out................................	______	______
c. Weighted average cost....................	______	______

Supporting calculations:

PROBLEM 7-4 ___, Concluded

4.

	FIFO	LIFO	Weighted Average
Sales			
Cost of merchandise sold			
Gross profit			
Inventory, __________, 2016			

Name ______________________________

PROBLEM 7-5 ___

1.

First-In, First-Out Method

Model	Quantity	Unit Cost	Total Cost

2.

Last-In, First-Out Method

Model	Quantity	Unit Cost	Total Cost

PROBLEM 7-5 ___, Concluded

3.

Weighted Average Cost Method

Model	Quantity	Unit Cost	Total Cost

4. a. ______________________

b. ______________________

PROBLEM 7-6 ___

	A	B	C	D	E	F	G
1	Inventory Sheet						
2	December 31, 2016						
3				Market Value per Unit (Net Realizable Value)	Total		
4							
5	Description	Inventory Quantity	Cost per Unit		Cost	Market	LCM
6							
7							
8							
9							
10							
11							
12							
13							
14							
15							
16							
17							
18							
19							
20							
21							
22							
23							
24							
25							
26							
27							
28							
29							
30							
31							
32							
33							
34							
35							

This Page Not Used.

APPENDIX PROBLEM 7-7 ___

1.

	A	B	C
1			
2		Cost	Retail
3			
4			
5			
6			
7			
8			
9			
10			
11			
12			
13			
14			
15			
16			
17			
18			

2.

	A	B	C
1			
2			Cost
3	a.		
4			
5			
6			
7			
8			
9			
10			
11			
12			
13			
14			
15			
16			
17	b.		
18			
19			
20			
21			
22			
23			
24			

This Page Not Used.

EXERCISE 8-1

EXERCISE 8-2

a.

b.

c.

EXERCISE 8-3

a.

b.

EXERCISE 8-3, Continued

c.

EXERCISE 8-3, Concluded

d.

EXERCISE 8-4

EXERCISE 8-5

EXERCISE 8-6

EXERCISE 8-7

EXERCISE 8-8

a.

b.

EXERCISE 8-9

a.

b.

EXERCISE 8-10

EXERCISE 8-11

a. ____

____

b. ____

____

EXERCISE 8-12

JOURNAL PAGE

	DATE		DESCRIPTION	POST. REF.	DEBIT	CREDIT	
1							1
2							2
3							3
4							4

EXERCISE 8-13

JOURNAL PAGE

	DATE		DESCRIPTION	POST. REF.	DEBIT	CREDIT	
1							1
2							2
3							3
4							4

EXERCISE 8-14

EXERCISE 8-15

EXERCISE 8-16

a. Addition to the balance per bank: ______________________

b. Deduction from the balance per bank: ______________________

c. Addition to the balance per company's records: ______________________

d. Deduction from the balance per company's records: ______________________

EXERCISE 8-17

EXERCISE 8-18

a.

Bank Reconciliation

b. ______________________________

____

c. ______________________________

____

EXERCISE 8-19

JOURNAL PAGE

	DATE		DESCRIPTION	POST. REF.	DEBIT	CREDIT	
1							1
2							2
3							3
4							4
5							5
6							6
7							7

EXERCISE 8-20

JOURNAL PAGE

	DATE		DESCRIPTION	POST. REF.	DEBIT	CREDIT	
1							1
2							2
3							3
4							4

EXERCISE 8-21

a.

Bank Reconciliation

b. ____

Name ______________________________

EXERCISE 8-22

EXERCISE 8-22, Concluded

(Optional)

Bank Reconciliation

Name ______________________________

EXERCISE 8-23

a. ______________________________

Bank Reconciliation

b. ______________________________

EXERCISE 8-24

a. and b.

JOURNAL PAGE

	DATE		DESCRIPTION	POST. REF.	DEBIT	CREDIT	
1							1
2							2
3							3
4							4
5							5
6							6
7							7
8							8
9							9

EXERCISE 8-25

EXERCISE 8-26

a. ______________________________

b. ______________________________

EXERCISE 8-27

a. ______________________________

b. ______________________________

c. ______________________________

EXERCISE 8-28

a. Year 3: ______________________________

Year 2: ______________________________

Year 1: ______________________________

b. Year 3: ______________________________

Year 2: ______________________________

Year 1: ______________________________

c. ______________________________

This Page Not Used.

Name ______________________________

PROBLEM 8-1 ___

This Page Not Used.

PROBLEM 8-2 ___

JOURNAL

PAGE

DATE		DESCRIPTION	POST. REF.	DEBIT	CREDIT

This Page Not Used.

PROBLEM 8-3 ___

1.

Bank Reconciliation

PROBLEM 8-3 ___, Concluded

2.

JOURNAL PAGE

	DATE		DESCRIPTION	POST. REF.	DEBIT	CREDIT	
1							1
2							2
3							3
4							4
5							5
6							6
7							7
8							8
9							9
10							10

3. ____

____

____

PROBLEM 8-4 ___

1.

Bank Reconciliation

PROBLEM 8-4 ___, Concluded

2.

JOURNAL

PAGE

	DATE		DESCRIPTION	POST. REF.	DEBIT	CREDIT	
1							1
2							2
3							3
4							4
5							5
6							6
7							7
8							8
9							9
10							10
11							11
12							12
13							13
14							14
15							15
16							16
17							17
18							18
19							19
20							20

3. ____

____

____

PROBLEM 8-5 ___

1.

Bank Reconciliation

PROBLEM 8-5 ___, Concluded

2.

JOURNAL

PAGE

	DATE	DESCRIPTION	POST. REF.	DEBIT	CREDIT	
1						1
2						2
3						3
4						4
5						5
6						6
7						7
8						8
9						9
10						10
11						11
12						12
13						13
14						14
15						15
16						16
17						17
18						18
19						19
20						20
21						21
22						22
23						23
24						24

3. ____

4. ____

____

____

____

____

____

EXERCISE 9-1

EXERCISE 9-2

a. MGM Resorts International:

b. Johnson & Johnson:

c.

EXERCISE 9-3

JOURNAL

PAGE

	DATE		DESCRIPTION	POST. REF.	DEBIT	CREDIT	
1							1
2							2
3							3
4							4
5							5
6							6
7							7
8							8
9							9
10							10
11							11
12							12
13							13
14							14
15							15
16							16
17							17
18							18
19							19
20							20

EXERCISE 9-4

JOURNAL

PAGE

	DATE		DESCRIPTION	POST. REF.	DEBIT	CREDIT	
1							1
2							2
3							3
4							4
5							5
6							6
7							7
8							8
9							9
10							10
11							11
12							12
13							13
14							14
15							15
16							16
17							17
18							18
19							19
20							20
21							21
22							22

EXERCISE 9-5

a. and b.

JOURNAL

PAGE

	DATE		DESCRIPTION	POST. REF.	DEBIT	CREDIT	
1							1
2							2
3							3
4							4
5							5
6							6
7							7
8							8

EXERCISE 9-6

a. ______________________

b. ______________________

c. ______________________

d. ______________________

EXERCISE 9-7

Account	Due Date	Number of Days Past Due
Avalanche Auto	August 8	
Bales Auto	October 11	
Derby Auto Repair	June 23	
Lucky's Auto Repair	September 2	
Pit Stop Auto	September 19	
Reliable Auto Repair	July 15	
Trident Auto	August 24	
Valley Repair & Tow	May 17	

EXERCISE 9-8

a.

Customer	Due Date	Number of Days Past Due
Builders Industries	May 1	
Elkhorn Company	June 20	
Granite Creek Inc.	July 13	
Lockwood Company	September 9	
Teton Company	August 7	

EXERCISE 9-8, Concluded

b.

	A	B	C	D	E	F	G
1	**Aging of Receivables Schedule**						
2	**August 31**						
3			**Not Past**	**Days Past Due**			
4	**Customer**	**Balance**	**Due**	**1–30**	**31–60**	**61–90**	**Over 90**
5	**Acme Industries Inc.**	**3,000**	**3,000**				
6	**Alliance Company**	**4,500**		**4,500**			
21	**Zollinger Company**	**5,000**			**5,000**		
22	**Subtotals**	**1,050,000**	**600,000**	**220,000**	**115,000**	**85,000**	**30,000**
23							
24							
25							
26							
27							
28							
29							
30							

EXERCISE 9-9

	BALANCE	NOT PAST DUE	DAYS PAST DUE			
			1–30	31–60	61–90	OVER 90

EXERCISE 9-10

JOURNAL PAGE

	DATE		DESCRIPTION	POST. REF.	DEBIT	CREDIT	
1							1
2							2
3							3
4							4
5							5
6							6
7							7

EXERCISE 9-11

		Estimated Uncollectible Accounts	
Age Interval	**Balance**	**Percent**	**Amount**
Not past due	$1,250,000	0.75%	$
1–30 days past due	500,000	3.00	
31–60 days past due	190,000	5.00	
61–90 days past due	60,000	15.00	
91–180 days past due	36,000	40.00	
Over 180 days past due	24,000	80.00	
Total	$2,060,000		$

EXERCISE 9-12

JOURNAL PAGE

	DATE		DESCRIPTION	POST. REF.	DEBIT	CREDIT	
1							1
2							2
3							3
4							4
5							5
6							6
7							7

EXERCISE 9-13

a.

JOURNAL PAGE

DATE		DESCRIPTION	POST. REF.	DEBIT	CREDIT

EXERCISE 9-13, Continued

b.

JOURNAL

PAGE

DATE		DESCRIPTION	POST. REF.	DEBIT	CREDIT

EXERCISE 9-13, Concluded

c.

____

____

____

EXERCISE 9-14

a.

JOURNAL

PAGE

	DATE		DESCRIPTION	POST. REF.	DEBIT	CREDIT	
1							1
2							2
3							3
4							4
5							5
6							6
7							7
8							8
9							9
10							10
11							11
12							12
13							13
14							14
15							15
16							16
17							17
18							18
19							19
20							20
21							21
22							22
23							23
24							24
25							25
26							26
27							27
28							28
29							29
30							30
31							31
32							32
33							33
34							34
35							35

EXERCISE 9-14, Continued

b.

JOURNAL

PAGE

	DATE		DESCRIPTION	POST. REF.	DEBIT	CREDIT	
1							1
2							2
3							3
4							4
5							5
6							6
7							7
8							8
9							9
10							10
11							11
12							12
13							13
14							14
15							15
16							16
17							17
18							18
19							19
20							20
21							21
22							22
23							23
24							24
25							25
26							26
27							27
28							28
29							29
30							30
31							31
32							32
33							33
34							34
35							35

EXERCISE 9-14, Concluded

Computations:

Aging Class (Number of Days Past Due)	Receivables Balance on December 31	Estimated Doubtful Accounts Percent	Estimated Doubtful Accounts Amount
0–30 days	$320,000	1%	$
31–60 days	110,000	3	
61–90 days	24,000	10	
91–120 days	18,000	33	
More than 120 days	43,000	75	
Total receivables	$515,000		
			$

c.

EXERCISE 9-15

EXERCISE 9-16

a. ______________________

b. ______________________

EXERCISE 9-17

a.

JOURNAL PAGE

	DATE		DESCRIPTION	POST. REF.	DEBIT	CREDIT	
1							1
2							2
3							3
4							4
5							5
6							6
7							7
8							8
9							9
10							10

b.

JOURNAL PAGE

	DATE		DESCRIPTION	POST. REF.	DEBIT	CREDIT	
1							1
2							2
3							3
4							4
5							5
6							6
7							7
8							8
9							9
10							10
11							11
12							12
13							13
14							14
15							15
16							16

EXERCISE 9-17, Concluded

c. ____

____

____

____

____

____

EXERCISE 9-18

a.

JOURNAL PAGE

	DATE		DESCRIPTION	POST. REF.	DEBIT	CREDIT	
1							1
2							2
3							3
4							4
5							5
6							6
7							7
8							8
9							9

EXERCISE 9-18, Concluded

b.

JOURNAL PAGE

	DATE		DESCRIPTION	POST. REF.	DEBIT	CREDIT	
1							1
2							2
3							3
4							4
5							5
6							6
7							7
8							8
9							9
10							10
11							11
12							12
13							13
14							14
15							15
16							16

Computations:

Aging Class (Number of Days Past Due)	Receivables Balance on December 31	Estimated Doubtful Accounts Percent	Estimated Doubtful Accounts Amount
0–30 days	$ 715,000	1%	$
31–60 days	310,000	2	
61–90 days	102,000	15	
91–120 days	76,000	30	
More than 120 days	97,000	60	
Total receivables	$1,300,000		
			$

EXERCISE 9-18, Concluded

c. ____

____

____

____

____

____

EXERCISE 9-19

	Date of Note	Face Amount	Interest Rate	Term of Note	Due Date	Interest Due
a.	January 3	$80,000	6%	120 days	______	$______
b.	February 20	27,000	4	30 days	______	______
c.	May 24	62,500	8	45 days	______	______
d.	August 30	30,000	5	90 days	______	______
e.	October 4	40,000	7	90 days	______	______

EXERCISE 9-20

a. ____

b. ____

c. (1) and (2)

JOURNAL PAGE

	DATE		DESCRIPTION	POST. REF.	DEBIT	CREDIT	
1							1
2							2
3							3
4							4
5							5
6							6
7							7

Name ______________________________

EXERCISE 9-21

1. ______________________________
2. ______________________________
3. ______________________________
4. ______________________________
5. ______________________________
6. ______________________________

   ____
7. ______________________________

   ____

EXERCISE 9-22

JOURNAL PAGE

	DATE		DESCRIPTION	POST. REF.	DEBIT	CREDIT	
1							1
2							2
3							3
4							4
5							5
6							6
7							7
8							8
9							9
10							10
11							11
12							12
13							13
14							14
15							15
16							16
17							17
18							18
19							19
20							20
21							21
22							22

EXERCISE 9-23

JOURNAL

PAGE

	DATE		DESCRIPTION	POST. REF.	DEBIT	CREDIT	
1							1
2							2
3							3
4							4
5							5
6							6
7							7
8							8
9							9
10							10
11							11
12							12
13							13
14							14
15							15

Name ______________________________

EXERCISE 9-24

JOURNAL

PAGE

	DATE		DESCRIPTION	POST. REF.	DEBIT	CREDIT	
1							1
2							2
3							3
4							4
5							5
6							6
7							7
8							8
9							9
10							10
11							11
12							12
13							13
14							14
15							15
16							16
17							17
18							18
19							19
20							20
21							21
22							22
23							23
24							24
25							25
26							26
27							27
28							28
29							29
30							30

EXERCISE 9-25

(Optional)

Balance Sheet

Name ______________________________

EXERCISE 9-26

a. and b.

	Year 2	Year 1
Sales		
Accounts receivable		
Average accounts receivable		
Accounts receivable turnover		
Average daily sales		
Days' sales in receivables		

c.

EXERCISE 9-27

a. and b.

	Year 2	**Year 1**
Sales		
Accounts receivable		
Average accounts receivable		
Accounts receivable turnover		
Average daily sales		
Days' sales in receivables		

c.

EXERCISE 9-28

a. and b.

	Year 2	**Year 1**
Sales	________	________
Accounts receivable	________	________
Average accounts receivable	________	________
Accounts receivable turnover	________	________
Average daily sales	________	________
Days' sales in receivables	________	________

c. ______________________________

EXERCISE 9-29

a. The Limited Brands Inc.: ______________________

H.J. Heinz Company: ______________________

b. ______________________

____

c. ______________________

PROBLEM 9-1 ___

1. and 2.

Allowance for Doubtful Accounts

Bad Debt Expense

3. ______________________________

4. a. ______________________________

b. ______________________________

c. ______________________________

PROBLEM 9-1 ___, Continued

2.

JOURNAL

PAGE

	DATE		DESCRIPTION	POST. REF.	DEBIT	CREDIT	
1							1
2							2
3							3
4							4
5							5
6							6
7							7
8							8
9							9
10							10
11							11
12							12
13							13
14							14
15							15
16							16
17							17
18							18
19							19
20							20
21							21
22							22
23							23
24							24
25							25
26							26
27							27
28							28
29							29
30							30
31							31
32							32
33							33
34							34
35							35

Name ____________________

PROBLEM 9-1 ___, Concluded

JOURNAL PAGE

DATE		DESCRIPTION	POST. REF.	DEBIT	CREDIT

This Page Not Used.

PROBLEM 9-2 ___

1.

Customer	Due Date	Number of Days Past Due

4.

JOURNAL PAGE

	DATE		DESCRIPTION	POST. REF.	DEBIT	CREDIT	
1							1
2							2
3							3
4							4
5							5
6							6
7							7

5. ______________________________

PROBLEM 9-2 ___, Concluded

2. and 3.

	A	B	C	D	E	F	G	H
1	**Aging of Receivables Schedule**							
2	**December 31, 2015**							
3			**Not Past**	**Days Past Due**				
4	**Customer**	**Balance**	**Due**	**1–30**	**31–60**	**61–90**	**91–120**	**Over 120**
5								
6								
30								
31	**Subtotals**							
32								
33								
34								
35								
36								
37								
38								
39								
40								
41								
42								
43								
44								
45								
46								

PROBLEM 9-3 ___

1.

Year	Bad Debt Expense: Expense Actually Reported	Bad Debt Expense: Expense Based on Estimate	Bad Debt Expense: Increase (Decrease) in Amount of Expense	Balance of Allowance Account, End of Year

2. ______________________

This Page Not Used.

PROBLEM 9-4 ___

1.

Note	(a) Due Date	(b) Interest Due at Maturity
1.		
2.		
3.		
4.		
5.		
6.		

2., 3., and 4.

JOURNAL PAGE

	DATE		DESCRIPTION	POST. REF.	DEBIT	CREDIT	
1							1
2							2
3							3
4							4
5							5
6							6
7							7
8							8
9							9
10							10
11							11
12							12
13							13
14							14
15							15
16							16
17							17
18							18
19							19
20							20
21							21
22							22
23							23
24							24

This Page Not Used.

PROBLEM 9-5 ___

JOURNAL

PAGE

DATE		DESCRIPTION	POST. REF.	DEBIT	CREDIT

This Page Not Used.

PROBLEM 9-6 ___

JOURNAL

PAGE

DATE		DESCRIPTION	POST. REF.	DEBIT	CREDIT

PROBLEM 9-6 ___, Concluded

JOURNAL

PAGE

DATE		DESCRIPTION	POST. REF.	DEBIT	CREDIT

EXERCISE 10-1

a. New printing press costs debited to the asset account: ____________________

b. Used printing press costs debited to the asset account: ____________________

EXERCISE 10-2

a. ____________________

b. ____________________

EXERCISE 10-3

EXERCISE 10-4

1. ______________________
2. ______________________
3. ______________________
4. ______________________
5. ______________________
6. ______________________
7. ______________________
8. ______________________
9. ______________________
10. ______________________

EXERCISE 10-5

1. ______________________
2. ______________________
3. ______________________
4. ______________________
5. ______________________
6. ______________________
7. ______________________
8. ______________________
9. ______________________
10. ______________________

Name ____________________

EXERCISE 10-6

JOURNAL PAGE

	DATE		DESCRIPTION	POST. REF.	DEBIT	CREDIT	
1							1
2							2
3							3
4							4
5							5
6							6
7							7
8							8
9							9
10							10
11							11
12							12

EXERCISE 10-7

a. ____________________

b. ____________________

EXERCISE 10-8

a. 4 years: ____________________

b. 8 years: ____________________

c. 10 years: ____________________

d. 16 years: ____________________

e. 25 years: ____________________

f. 40 years: ____________________

g. 50 years: ____________________

EXERCISE 10-9

____

____

EXERCISE 10-10

____

____

____

____

EXERCISE 10-11

a.

Truck No.	Rate per Mile	Miles Operated	Credit to Accumulated Depreciation
1	________	________	$________
2	________	________	$________
3	________	________	$________
4	________	________	$________
Total			$________

b.

JOURNAL PAGE

	DATE		DESCRIPTION	POST. REF.	DEBIT	CREDIT	
1							1
2							2
3							3
4							4
5							5

EXERCISE 10-12

a. Straight-line method:

First year: ____

Second year: ____

b. Double-declining-balance method:

First year: ____

Second year: ____

EXERCISE 10-13

a. Straight-line method:

____

b. Double-declining-balance method:

Year 1: ______________________

Year 2: ______________________

EXERCISE 10-14

a. Straight-line method:

Year 1: ______________________

Year 2: ______________________

b. Double-declining-balance method:

Year 1: ______________________

Year 2: ______________________

EXERCISE 10-15

a. ______________________

b. ______________________

c. ______________________

EXERCISE 10-16

a. and b.

JOURNAL PAGE

	DATE		DESCRIPTION	POST. REF.	DEBIT	CREDIT	
1							1
2							2
3							3
4							4
5							5
6							6
7							7
8							8
9							9
10							10

EXERCISE 10-17

a.

b. (1) and (2)

JOURNAL PAGE

	DATE		DESCRIPTION	POST. REF.	DEBIT	CREDIT	
1							1
2							2
3							3
4							4
5							5
6							6
7							7
8							8
9							9
10							10
11							11
12							12
13							13
14							14

EXERCISE 10-18

a. 2013: ______________________

2014: ______________________

2015: ______________________

b. ______________________

EXERCISE 10-18, Concluded

c. and d.

JOURNAL PAGE

	DATE		DESCRIPTION	POST. REF.	DEBIT	CREDIT	
1							1
2							2
3							3
4							4
5							5
6							6
7							7
8							8
9							9
10							10
11							11
12							12

EXERCISE 10-19

a. ____

____

b.

JOURNAL PAGE

	DATE		DESCRIPTION	POST. REF.	DEBIT	CREDIT	
1							1
2							2
3							3
4							4
5							5

EXERCISE 10-20

a. ______________________________________

____

b.

JOURNAL PAGE

	DATE		DESCRIPTION	POST. REF.	DEBIT	CREDIT	
1							1
2							2
3							3
4							4
5							5

EXERCISE 10-21

a.

	CURRENT YEAR	PRECEDING YEAR

EXERCISE 10-21, Concluded

b.

EXERCISE 10-22

EXERCISE 10-23

a.

EXERCISE 10-23, Concluded

b. ______________________________

EXERCISE 10-24

a. Best Buy: ______________________________

RadioShack: ______________________________

b. ______________________________

APPENDIX EXERCISE 10-25

a.

b.

APPENDIX EXERCISE 10-26

a.

b.

APPENDIX EXERCISE 10-27

a. and b.

JOURNAL PAGE

	DATE		DESCRIPTION	POST. REF.	DEBIT	CREDIT	
1							1
2							2
3							3
4							4
5							5
6							6
7							7
8							8
9							9
10							10
11							11
12							12
13							13
14							14

APPENDIX EXERCISE 10-28

a. and b.

JOURNAL

PAGE

	DATE		DESCRIPTION	POST. REF.	DEBIT	CREDIT	
1							1
2							2
3							3
4							4
5							5
6							6
7							7
8							8
9							9
10							10
11							11
12							12
13							13
14							14

Name ______________________________

PROBLEM 10-1 ___

1. and 2.

Item	Land	Land Improvements	Building	Other Accounts
a.				
b.				
c.				
d.				
e.				
f.				
g.				
h.				
i.				
j.				
k.				
l.				
m.				
n.				
o.				
p.				
q.				
r.				
s.				
Total				

PROBLEM 10-1 ___, Concluded

3. ______________________________

4. ______________________________

Name ______________________

PROBLEM 10-2 ___

1.

	Depreciation Expense		
Year	**a. Straight-Line Method**	**b. Units-of-Output Method**	**c. Double-Declining-Balance Method**
____	____	____	____
____	____	____	____
____	____	____	____
____	____	____	____
Total	____	____	____

Supporting Calculations:

2.

3.

This Page Not Used.

PROBLEM 10-3 ___

a.

Straight-Line Method

Year	Calculations	Depreciation Expense
2014		
2015		
2016		
2017		

b.

Units-of-Output Method

Year	Calculations	Depreciation Expense
2014		
2015		
2016		
2017		

c.

Double-Declining-Balance Method

Year	Calculations	Depreciation Expense
2014		
2015		
2016		
2017		

This Page Not Used.

PROBLEM 10-4 ___

1. a.

Straight-Line Method

Year	Depreciation Expense	Accumulated Depreciation, End of Year	Book Value, End of Year
1			
2			
3			
4			
5			

b.

Double-Declining-Balance Method

Year	Depreciation Expense	Accumulated Depreciation, End of Year	Book Value, End of Year
1			
2			
3			
4			
5			

PROBLEM 10-4 ___, Concluded

2.

JOURNAL

PAGE

	DATE		DESCRIPTION	POST. REF.	DEBIT	CREDIT	
1							1
2							2
3							3
4							4
5							5
6							6
7							7

3.

JOURNAL

PAGE

	DATE		DESCRIPTION	POST. REF.	DEBIT	CREDIT	
1							1
2							2
3							3
4							4
5							5
6							6
7							7

PROBLEM 10-5 ___

JOURNAL

PAGE

DATE		DESCRIPTION	POST. REF.	DEBIT	CREDIT

PROBLEM 10-5 ___, Concluded

JOURNAL

PAGE

DATE		DESCRIPTION	POST. REF.	DEBIT	CREDIT

PROBLEM 10-6 ___

1. a. ____

____

____

b. ____

____

____

c. ____

____

____

2.

JOURNAL

PAGE

	DATE		DESCRIPTION	POST. REF.	DEBIT	CREDIT	
1							1
2							2
3							3
4							4
5							5
6							6
7							7
8							8
9							9
10							10
11							11
12							12
13							13
14							14
15							15

This Page Not Used.

EXERCISE 11-1

EXERCISE 11-2

a. and b.

JOURNAL PAGE

	DATE		DESCRIPTION	POST. REF.	DEBIT	CREDIT	
1							1
2							2
3							3
4							4
5							5
6							6
7							7
8							8
9							9
10							10
11							11
12							12
13							13
14							14
15							15

EXERCISE 11-3

a. ______________________

____

b. (1) ______________________

____

(2) ______________________

____

c. ______________________

EXERCISE 11-4

a. and b.

JOURNAL PAGE

	DATE		DESCRIPTION	POST. REF.	DEBIT	CREDIT	
1							1
2							2
3							3
4							4
5							5
6							6
7							7

EXERCISE 11-5

a. and b.

JOURNAL PAGE

	DATE		DESCRIPTION	POST. REF.	DEBIT	CREDIT	
1							1
2							2
3							3
4							4
5							5
6							6
7							7
8							8

EXERCISE 11-6

a., b., and c.

JOURNAL PAGE

	DATE		DESCRIPTION	POST. REF.	DEBIT	CREDIT	
1							1
2							2
3							3
4							4
5							5
6							6
7							7
8							8
9							9
10							10
11							11
12							12
13							13
14							14
15							15

EXERCISE 11-7

a. ______________________________

____

b. ______________________________

____

c. ______________________________

____

EXERCISE 11-8

a.

b.

EXERCISE 11-9

	Consultant	Computer Programmer	Administrator
Regular earnings	$	$	$
Overtime earnings			
Gross pay	$	$	$
Less: Social security tax	$	$	$
Medicare tax			
Federal income tax withheld			
	$	$	$
Net pay	$	$	$

EXERCISE 11-9, Concluded

Withholding Supporting Calculations:

	CONSULTANT	COMPUTER PROGRAMMER	ADMINISTRATOR

EXERCISE 11-10

a.

EXERCISE 11-10, Concluded

b. and c.

JOURNAL PAGE

	DATE		DESCRIPTION	POST. REF.	DEBIT	CREDIT	
1							1
2							2
3							3
4							4
5							5
6							6
7							7
8							8
9							9
10							10
11							11
12							12
13							13
14							14
15							15
16							16

EXERCISE 11-11

a.

EXERCISE 11-11, Concluded

b.

JOURNAL PAGE

DATE		DESCRIPTION	POST. REF.	DEBIT	CREDIT

EXERCISE 11-12

a. and b.

JOURNAL PAGE

DATE		DESCRIPTION	POST. REF.	DEBIT	CREDIT

EXERCISE 11-13

a. and b.

JOURNAL PAGE

	DATE		DESCRIPTION	POST. REF.	DEBIT	CREDIT	
1							1
2							2
3							3
4							4
5							5
6							6
7							7
8							8
9							9
10							10
11							11
12							12
13							13
14							14
15							15
16							16
17							17
18							18

EXERCISE 11-14

EXERCISE 11-15

a.

b.

c.

d.

e.

EXERCISE 11-16

a.

JOURNAL PAGE

	DATE		DESCRIPTION	POST. REF.	DEBIT	CREDIT	
1							1
2							2
3							3
4							4
5							5

EXERCISE 11-16, Concluded

b.

EXERCISE 11-17

a.

JOURNAL PAGE

	DATE		DESCRIPTION	POST. REF.	DEBIT	CREDIT	
1							1
2							2
3							3
4							4
5							5
6							6
7							7

b.

EXERCISE 11-18

EXERCISE 11-19

a. and b.

JOURNAL PAGE

	DATE		DESCRIPTION	POST. REF.	DEBIT	CREDIT	
1							1
2							2
3							3
4							4
5							5
6							6
7							7
8							8
9							9
10							10

EXERCISE 11-20

a.

b.

JOURNAL PAGE

	DATE		DESCRIPTION	POST. REF.	DEBIT	CREDIT	
1							1
2							2
3							3
4							4

c.

EXERCISE 11-21

a.

JOURNAL PAGE

	DATE		DESCRIPTION	POST. REF.	DEBIT	CREDIT	
1							1
2							2
3							3
4							4
5							5

EXERCISE 11-21, Concluded

b. ______________________________

EXERCISE 11-22

a. Previous year: ______________________________

Current year: ______________________________

b. ______________________________

EXERCISE 11-23

a.

	Apple Inc:	Dell, Inc.:
Quick Ratio:	______________	______________

Computations:

b.

PROBLEM 11-1 ___

1.

JOURNAL

PAGE

	DATE		DESCRIPTION	POST. REF.	DEBIT	CREDIT	
1							1
2							2
3							3
4							4
5							5
6							6
7							7
8							8
9							9
10							10
11							11
12							12
13							13
14							14
15							15
16							16
17							17
18							18
19							19
20							20
21							21
22							22
23							23
24							24
25							25
26							26
27							27
28							28
29							29
30							30
31							31
32							32
33							33
34							34
35							35

PROBLEM 11-1 ___, Continued

JOURNAL

PAGE

DATE		DESCRIPTION	POST. REF.	DEBIT	CREDIT

PROBLEM 11-1 ___, Concluded

2.

JOURNAL

PAGE

	DATE		DESCRIPTION	POST. REF.	DEBIT	CREDIT	
1							1
2							2
3							3
4							4
5							5
6							6
7							7
8							8
9							9
10							10
11							11
12							12
13							13
14							14
15							15
16							16
17							17
18							18
19							19
20							20
21							21
22							22
23							23
24							24
25							25
26							26
27							27
28							28
29							29
30							30
31							31
32							32
33							33
34							34
35							35

This Page Not Used.

PROBLEM 11-2 ___

1.

JOURNAL

PAGE

	DATE		DESCRIPTION	POST. REF.	DEBIT	CREDIT	
1							1
2							2
3							3
4							4
5							5
6							6
7							7
8							8
9							9
10							10
11							11
12							12
13							13
14							14
15							15
16							16
17							17
18							18
19							19
20							20
21							21
22							22
23							23
24							24
25							25
26							26
27							27
28							28
29							29
30							30
31							31
32							32
33							33
34							34
35							35

PROBLEM 11-2 ___, Concluded

2.

JOURNAL

PAGE

	DATE		DESCRIPTION	POST. REF.	DEBIT	CREDIT	
1							1
2							2
3							3
4							4
5							5
6							6
7							7
8							8
9							9
10							10
11							11
12							12
13							13
14							14
15							15
16							16
17							17
18							18
19							19
20							20
21							21
22							22
23							23
24							24
25							25
26							26
27							27
28							28
29							29
30							30
31							31
32							32
33							33
34							34
35							35

Name ________________________________

PROBLEM 11-3 ___

1.

Employee	Gross Earnings	Federal Income Tax Withheld	Social Security Tax Withheld	Medicare Tax Withheld

PROBLEM 11-3 ___, Concluded

2. Payroll taxes incurred and paid by employer:

   a. Social security tax paid by employer .... $ ______________

   b. Medicare tax paid by employer .... ______________

   c. State unemployment compensation tax .... ______________

   Calculations and comments:

   ____

   ____

   ____

   ____

   ____

   ____

   ____

   ____

   d. Federal unemployment compensation tax .... ______________

   e. Total payroll tax expense .... $ ______________

PROBLEM 11-4 ___

1.

PAYROLL FOR WEEK ENDING *December 9, 2016*

	EMPLOYEE NAME	TOTAL HOURS	EARNINGS			DEDUCTIONS					PAID		ACCOUNTS DEBITED		
			REGULAR	OVERTIME	TOTAL	SOCIAL SECURITY TAX	MEDICARE TAX	FEDERAL INCOME TAX	U.S. SAVINGS BONDS	TOTAL	NET PAY	CK. NO.	SALES SALARIES EXPENSE	OFFICE SALARIES EXPENSE	
1															1
2															2
3															3
4															4
5															5
6															6
7															7
8															8
9															9
10															10
11															11
12															12

PROBLEM 11-4 ___, Concluded

2.

JOURNAL

PAGE

	DATE		DESCRIPTION	POST. REF.	DEBIT	CREDIT	
1							1
2							2
3							3
4							4
5							5
6							6
7							7
8							8
9							9
10							10

Name ____________________________

PROBLEM 11-5 ___

1.

JOURNAL

PAGE

	DATE		DESCRIPTION	POST. REF.	DEBIT	CREDIT	
1							1
2							2
3							3
4							4
5							5
6							6
7							7
8							8
9							9
10							10
11							11
12							12
13							13
14							14
15							15
16							16
17							17
18							18
19							19
20							20
21							21
22							22
23							23
24							24
25							25
26							26
27							27
28							28
29							29
30							30
31							31
32							32
33							33
34							34
35							35

PROBLEM 11-5 ___, Continued

JOURNAL

PAGE

DATE		DESCRIPTION	POST. REF.	DEBIT	CREDIT

PROBLEM 11-5 ___, Continued

JOURNAL

PAGE

	DATE		DESCRIPTION	POST. REF.	DEBIT	CREDIT	
1							1
2							2
3							3
4							4
5							5
6							6
7							7
8							8
9							9
10							10
11							11
12							12
13							13
14							14
15							15
16							16
17							17
18							18
19							19
20							20
21							21
22							22
23							23
24							24
25							25
26							26
27							27
28							28
29							29
30							30
31							31
32							32
33							33
34							34
35							35
36							36

PROBLEM 11-5 ___, Concluded

2.

JOURNAL

PAGE

	DATE		DESCRIPTION	POST. REF.	DEBIT	CREDIT	
1							1
2							2
3							3
4							4
5							5
6							6
7							7
8							8
9							9
10							10
11							11
12							12
13							13
14							14
15							15
16							16
17							17
18							18
19							19
20							20
21							21
22							22
23							23
24							24
25							25
26							26
27							27
28							28
29							29
30							30
31							31
32							32
33							33
34							34
35							35

COMPREHENSIVE PROBLEM 3

1.

JOURNAL

PAGE

	DATE		DESCRIPTION	POST. REF.	DEBIT	CREDIT	
1							1
2							2
3							3
4							4
5							5
6							6
7							7
8							8
9							9
10							10
11							11
12							12
13							13
14							14
15							15
16							16
17							17
18							18
19							19
20							20
21							21
22							22
23							23
24							24
25							25
26							26
27							27
28							28
29							29
30							30
31							31
32							32
33							33
34							34
35							35

COMPREHENSIVE PROBLEM 3, Continued

JOURNAL

PAGE

	DATE		DESCRIPTION	POST. REF.	DEBIT	CREDIT	
1							1
2							2
3							3
4							4
5							5
6							6
7							7
8							8
9							9
10							10
11							11
12							12
13							13
14							14
15							15
16							16
17							17
18							18
19							19
20							20
21							21
22							22
23							23
24							24
25							25
26							26
27							27
28							28
29							29
30							30
31							31
32							32
33							33
34							34
35							35
36							36

COMPREHENSIVE PROBLEM 3, Continued

JOURNAL

PAGE

	DATE		DESCRIPTION	POST. REF.	DEBIT	CREDIT	
1							1
2							2
3							3
4							4
5							5
6							6
7							7
8							8
9							9
10							10
11							11
12							12
13							13
14							14
15							15
16							16
17							17
18							18
19							19
20							20
21							21
22							22
23							23
24							24
25							25
26							26
27							27
28							28
29							29
30							30
31							31
32							32
33							33
34							34
35							35
36							36

COMPREHENSIVE PROBLEM 3, Continued

2.

Bank Reconciliation

3.

JOURNAL PAGE

	DATE		DESCRIPTION	POST. REF.	DEBIT	CREDIT	
1							1
2							2
3							3
4							4
5							5

COMPREHENSIVE PROBLEM 3, Continued

4.

JOURNAL

PAGE

	DATE		DESCRIPTION	POST. REF.	DEBIT	CREDIT	
1							1
2							2
3							3
4							4
5							5
6							6
7							7
8							8
9							9
10							10
11							11
12							12
13							13
14							14
15							15
16							16
17							17
18							18
19							19
20							20
21							21
22							22
23							23
24							24
25							25
26							26
27							27
28							28
29							29
30							30
31							31
32							32
33							33
34							34
35							35

COMPREHENSIVE PROBLEM 3, Continued

JOURNAL

PAGE

DATE		DESCRIPTION	POST. REF.	DEBIT	CREDIT

COMPREHENSIVE PROBLEM 3, Continued

5.

Balance Sheet

COMPREHENSIVE PROBLEM 3, Concluded

Balance Sheet

EXERCISE 12-1

JOURNAL

PAGE

	DATE		DESCRIPTION	POST. REF.	DEBIT	CREDIT	
1							1
2							2
3							3
4							4
5							5
6							6
7							7

EXERCISE 12-2

JOURNAL

PAGE

	DATE		DESCRIPTION	POST. REF.	DEBIT	CREDIT	
1							1
2							2
3							3
4							4
5							5
6							6
7							7
8							8
9							9

EXERCISE 12-3

	Taylor	Albright
a.		
b.		
c.		
d.		
e.		

Details:

	Taylor	Albright	Total
a.			
b.			
c.			
d.			
e.			

EXERCISE 12-4

	Taylor	Albright
a.		
b.		
c.		
d.		
e.		

Details:

	Taylor	Albright	Total
a.			
b.			
c.			
d.			
e.			

EXERCISE 12-5

	Leigh Meadows	Luke Kowalski	Total

EXERCISE 12-6

a. ______________________________

b. ______________________________

EXERCISE 12-7

a.

	Farley	Clark	Total

b. (1) and (2)

JOURNAL PAGE

	DATE		DESCRIPTION	POST. REF.	DEBIT	CREDIT	
1							1
2							2
3							3
4							4
5							5
6							6
7							7
8							8
9							9
10							10

c. ______________________________

EXERCISE 12-8

a.

	WLKT Partners	Madison Sanders	Observer Newspaper, LLC	Total

b.

JOURNAL PAGE

	DATE		DESCRIPTION	POST. REF.	DEBIT	CREDIT	
1							1
2							2
3							3
4							4
5							5
6							6
7							7
8							8
9							9
10							10
11							11
12							12
13							13
14							14
15							15
16							16
17							17
18							18
19							19
20							20

EXERCISE 12-8, Concluded

c.

Statement of Members' Equity

	WLKT PARTNERS	MADISON SANDERS	OBSERVER NEWSPAPER, LLC	TOTAL

d.

EXERCISE 12-9

a., b., and c.

JOURNAL PAGE

	DATE		DESCRIPTION	POST. REF.	DEBIT	CREDIT	
1							1
2							2
3							3
4							4
5							5
6							6
7							7
8							8
9							9
10							10

d. ____

EXERCISE 12-10

a. and b.

JOURNAL PAGE

	DATE		DESCRIPTION	POST. REF.	DEBIT	CREDIT	
1							1
2							2
3							3
4							4

EXERCISE 12-11

a. (1) and (2)

JOURNAL PAGE

	DATE		DESCRIPTION	POST. REF.	DEBIT	CREDIT	
1							1
2							2
3							3
4							4
5							5
6							6
7							7
8							8

b.

EXERCISE 12-12

a.

JOURNAL PAGE

	DATE		DESCRIPTION	POST. REF.	DEBIT	CREDIT	
1							1
2							2
3							3
4							4
5							5

b.

EXERCISE 12-12, Concluded

c.

EXERCISE 12-13

a.

b.

JOURNAL PAGE

	DATE		DESCRIPTION	POST. REF.	DEBIT	CREDIT	
1							1
2							2
3							3
4							4
5							5

EXERCISE 12-13, Concluded

c.

EXERCISE 12-14

a.

JOURNAL PAGE

	DATE		DESCRIPTION	POST. REF.	DEBIT	CREDIT	
1							1
2							2
3							3
4							4

b. (1)

JOURNAL PAGE

	DATE		DESCRIPTION	POST. REF.	DEBIT	CREDIT	
1							1
2							2
3							3
4							4
5							5

EXERCISE 12-14, Concluded

Supporting calculations for the bonus:

(2)

JOURNAL PAGE

	DATE		DESCRIPTION	POST. REF.	DEBIT	CREDIT	
1							1
2							2
3							3
4							4
5							5

Supporting calculations for the bonus:

EXERCISE 12-15

a.

JOURNAL PAGE

	DATE		DESCRIPTION	POST. REF.	DEBIT	CREDIT	
1							1
2							2
3							3
4							4

b. (1)

JOURNAL PAGE

	DATE		DESCRIPTION	POST. REF.	DEBIT	CREDIT	
1							1
2							2
3							3
4							4
5							5

Supporting calculations for the bonus:

(2)

JOURNAL PAGE

	DATE		DESCRIPTION	POST. REF.	DEBIT	CREDIT	
1							1
2							2
3							3
4							4
5							5

EXERCISE 12-15, Concluded

Supporting calculations for the bonus:

EXERCISE 12-16

Statement of Partnership Equity

	DENNIS OVERTON, CAPITAL	BEN TESTERMAN, CAPITAL	RANDY CAMPBELL, CAPITAL	TOTAL PARTNERSHIP CAPITAL

EXERCISE 12-16, Continued

Calculations

Admission of Randy Campbell:

Net income distribution:

EXERCISE 12-16, Concluded

Withdrawals:

____

____

____

____

____

____

EXERCISE 12-17

a. and b.

JOURNAL PAGE

	DATE		DESCRIPTION	POST. REF.	DEBIT	CREDIT	
1							1
2							2
3							3
4							4
5							5
6							6
7							7
8							8
9							9
10							10
11							11
12							12

EXERCISE 12-18

a. through f.

EXERCISE 12-18, Concluded

EXERCISE 12-19

a.

b. and c.

	HEWITT	PATEL

Name ______________________________

EXERCISE 12-20

	OLIVER	ANSARI	TOTAL

EXERCISE 12-21

a. ______________________________

b. ______________________________

____

c.

JOURNAL PAGE

	DATE		DESCRIPTION	POST. REF.	DEBIT	CREDIT	
1							1
2							2
3							3

Supporting calculations:

	LEWIS	ZAPATA	FOWLER

EXERCISE 12-22

a.

	BRAY	LINCOLN	MAPES	TOTAL

b.

	BRAY	LINCOLN	MAPES	TOTAL

EXERCISE 12-23

	NETTLES	KING	TANAKA

EXERCISE 12-24

Statement of Partnership Liquidation

	CASH	NONCASH ASSETS	LIABILITIES	CAPITAL		
				GOLD	PORTER	SIMS

Name ______________________

EXERCISE 12-25

a.

Statement of LLC Liquidation

	CASH	NONCASH ASSETS	LIABILITIES	MEMBER EQUITY		
				LESTER	TORRES	HEARST

EXERCISE 12-25, Concluded

b.

JOURNAL PAGE

	DATE		DESCRIPTION	POST. REF.	DEBIT	CREDIT	
1							1
2							2
3							3
4							4
5							5

c.

EXERCISE 12-26

a. (1) and (2)

JOURNAL PAGE

	DATE		DESCRIPTION	POST. REF.	DEBIT	CREDIT	
1							1
2							2
3							3
4							4
5							5
6							6
7							7
8							8
9							9
10							10

b.

Statement of Partnership Equity

	ANGEL ALVAREZ	EMMA ALLISON	TOTAL

EXERCISE 12-27

a.

b.

EXERCISE 12-28

a.

b.

PROBLEM 12-1 ___

1.

JOURNAL

PAGE

	DATE		DESCRIPTION	POST. REF.	DEBIT	CREDIT	
1							1
2							2
3							3
4							4
5							5
6							6
7							7
8							8
9							9
10							10
11							11
12							12
13							13
14							14
15							15

PROBLEM 12-1 ___, Continued

2.

Balance Sheet

PROBLEM 12-1 ___, Concluded

3.

JOURNAL PAGE

	DATE		DESCRIPTION	POST. REF.	DEBIT	CREDIT	
1							1
2							2
3							3
4							4
5							5
6							6
7							7
8							8
9							9
10							10

Computations:

This Page Not Used.

PROBLEM 12-2 ___

Plan	(1) Net Income of ____________		(2) Net Income of ____________	
	Partner: ________	Partner: ________	Partner: ________	Partner: ________
a.				
b.				
c.				
d.				
e.				
f.				

PROBLEM 12-2 ___, Concluded

Supporting calculations:

	NET INCOME OF ________		NET INCOME OF ________	

PROBLEM 12-3 ___

1.

Income Statement

Division of net income:

PROBLEM 12-3 ___, Continued

2.

Statement of Partnership Equity

PROBLEM 12-3 ___, Concluded

3.

Balance Sheet

This Page Not Used.

PROBLEM 12-4 ___

1. and 2.

JOURNAL

PAGE

	DATE		DESCRIPTION	POST. REF.	DEBIT	CREDIT	
1							1
2							2
3							3
4							4
5							5
6							6
7							7
8							8
9							9
10							10
11							11
12							12
13							13
14							14
15							15
16							16
17							17
18							18
19							19
20							20
21							21
22							22
23							23
24							24
25							25
26							26
27							27
28							28
29							29
30							30
31							31
32							32
33							33
34							34
35							35

PROBLEM 12-4 ___, Concluded

3.

Balance Sheet

PROBLEM 12-5 ___

1.

Statement of Partnership Liquidation

	CASH	NONCASH ASSETS	LIABILITIES	CAPITAL		

PROBLEM 12-5___, Concluded

2. a.

JOURNAL

PAGE

	DATE		DESCRIPTION	POST. REF.	DEBIT	CREDIT	
1							1
2							2
3							3
4							4

b.

JOURNAL

PAGE

	DATE		DESCRIPTION	POST. REF.	DEBIT	CREDIT	
1							1
2							2
3							3
4							4

 Name ____________________

PROBLEM 12-6 ___

1. a.

Statement of Partnership Liquidation

	CASH	NONCASH ASSETS	LIABILITIES	CAPITAL		

Name ______________________

PROBLEM 12-6 ___, Continued

b.

Statement of Partnership Liquidation

	CASH	NONCASH ASSETS	LIABILITIES	CAPITAL		

PROBLEM 12-6 ___, Concluded

2. a.

JOURNAL PAGE

	DATE		DESCRIPTION	POST. REF.	DEBIT	CREDIT	
1							1
2							2
3							3
4							4

b.

JOURNAL PAGE

	DATE		DESCRIPTION	POST. REF.	DEBIT	CREDIT	
1							1
2							2
3							3
4							4

This Page Not Used.

EXERCISE 13-1

Description	1st Year	2nd Year	3rd Year	4th Year
Total dividend declared				
Preferred dividend (current)				
Preferred dividend in arrears				
Total preferred dividends				
Preferred shares outstanding				
Preferred dividend per share				
Dividend for common shares				
Common shares outstanding				
Common dividend per share				

EXERCISE 13-2

Description	1st Year	2nd Year	3rd Year	4th Year
Total dividend declared				
Preferred dividend (current)				
Preferred dividend in arrears				
Total preferred dividends				
Preferred shares outstanding				
Preferred dividend per share				
Dividend for common shares				
Common shares outstanding				
Common dividend per share				

EXERCISE 13-3

a.

JOURNAL PAGE

	DATE		DESCRIPTION	POST. REF.	DEBIT	CREDIT	
1							1
2							2
3							3
4							4
5							5
6							6
7							7
8							8
9							9
10							10
11							11
12							12
13							13

b. ____

EXERCISE 13-4

a.

JOURNAL PAGE

	DATE		DESCRIPTION	POST. REF.	DEBIT	CREDIT	
1							1
2							2
3							3
4							4
5							5
6							6
7							7
8							8
9							9
10							10
11							11
12							12
13							13

b. ____

EXERCISE 13-5

JOURNAL PAGE

	DATE		DESCRIPTION	POST. REF.	DEBIT	CREDIT	
1							1
2							2
3							3
4							4
5							5
6							6
7							7

EXERCISE 13-6

a., b., and c.

JOURNAL PAGE

	DATE		DESCRIPTION	POST. REF.	DEBIT	CREDIT	
1							1
2							2
3							3
4							4
5							5
6							6
7							7
8							8
9							9
10							10
11							11
12							12
13							13
14							14
15							15
16							16
17							17
18							18

EXERCISE 13-7

JOURNAL

PAGE

	DATE		DESCRIPTION	POST. REF.	DEBIT	CREDIT	
1							1
2							2
3							3
4							4
5							5
6							6
7							7
8							8
9							9
10							10
11							11
12							12
13							13
14							14
15							15
16							16
17							17
18							18

EXERCISE 13-8

JOURNAL

PAGE

DATE		DESCRIPTION	POST. REF.	DEBIT	CREDIT

EXERCISE 13-9

JOURNAL PAGE

	DATE		DESCRIPTION	POST. REF.	DEBIT	CREDIT	
1							1
2							2
3							3
4							4
5							5
6							6
7							7
8							8
9							9

EXERCISE 13-10

a. (1) and (2)

JOURNAL PAGE

	DATE		DESCRIPTION	POST. REF.	DEBIT	CREDIT	
1							1
2							2
3							3
4							4
5							5
6							6
7							7
8							8
9							9
10							10

b. **(1)** Total paid-in capital: ______________________________

(2) Total retained earnings: ______________________________

(3) Total stockholders' equity: ______________________________

c. **(1)** Total paid-in capital: ______________________________

(2) Total retained earnings: ______________________________

(3) Total stockholders' equity: ______________________________

EXERCISE 13-11

a.

JOURNAL PAGE

	DATE		DESCRIPTION	POST. REF.	DEBIT	CREDIT	
1							1
2							2
3							3
4							4
5							5
6							6
7							7
8							8
9							9
10							10
11							11
12							12
13							13
14							14
15							15
16							16
17							17
18							18

b. ______________________________

c. ______________________________

EXERCISE 13-12

a.

JOURNAL

PAGE

	DATE		DESCRIPTION	POST. REF.	DEBIT	CREDIT	
1							1
2							2
3							3
4							4
5							5
6							6
7							7
8							8
9							9
10							10
11							11
12							12
13							13
14							14
15							15
16							16
17							17
18							18

b. ______________________________

c. ______________________________

d. ______________________________

____

____

EXERCISE 13-13

a.

JOURNAL

PAGE

	DATE		DESCRIPTION	POST. REF.	DEBIT	CREDIT	
1							1
2							2
3							3
4							4
5							5
6							6
7							7
8							8
9							9
10							10
11							11
12							12
13							13
14							14
15							15
16							16
17							17
18							18

b. ____________________

c. ____________________

d. ____________________

EXERCISE 13-14

EXERCISE 13-15

EXERCISE 13-16

EXERCISE 13-17

Retained Earnings Statement

EXERCISE 13-18

EXERCISE 13-18, Concluded

(Optional)

EXERCISE 13-19

Statement of Stockholders' Equity

EXERCISE 13-20

a. ____________________

b. ____________________

EXERCISE 13-21

	Assets	Liabilities	Stockholders' Equity
(1) Authorizing and issuing stock certificates in a stock split	______	______	______
(2) Declaring a stock dividend	______	______	______
(3) Issuing stock certificates for the stock dividend declared in (2)	______	______	______
(4) Declaring a cash dividend	______	______	______
(5) Paying the cash dividend declared in (4)	______	______	______

EXERCISE 13-22

JOURNAL

PAGE

DATE		DESCRIPTION	POST. REF.	DEBIT	CREDIT

EXERCISE 13-23

EXERCISE 13-24

a.

EXERCISE 13-24, Concluded

b.

	YEAR 3	YEAR 2	YEAR 1

EXERCISE 13-25

a. OfficeMax: ______________________

Staples: ______________________

b. ______________________

This Page Not Used.

PROBLEM 13-1 ___

1.

Year	Total Dividends	Preferred Dividends		Common Dividends	
		Total	Per Share	Total	Per Share
2011					
2012					
2013					
2014					
2015					
2016					

2. Average annual dividend for preferred: ________________________________

Average annual dividend for common: ________________________________

3. a. ________________________________

b. ________________________________

This Page Not Used.

PROBLEM 13-2 ___

JOURNAL

PAGE

	DATE		DESCRIPTION	POST. REF.	DEBIT	CREDIT	
1							1
2							2
3							3
4							4
5							5
6							6
7							7
8							8
9							9
10							10
11							11
12							12
13							13
14							14
15							15
16							16
17							17
18							18
19							19
20							20
21							21
22							22
23							23
24							24
25							25
26							26
27							27
28							28
29							29
30							30
31							31
32							32
33							33
34							34
35							35
36							36

This Page Not Used.

PROBLEM 13-3 ___

a. through g.

JOURNAL

PAGE

	DATE		DESCRIPTION	POST. REF.	DEBIT	CREDIT	
1							1
2							2
3							3
4							4
5							5
6							6
7							7
8							8
9							9
10							10
11							11
12							12
13							13
14							14
15							15
16							16
17							17
18							18
19							19
20							20
21							21
22							22
23							23
24							24
25							25
26							26
27							27
28							28
29							29
30							30
31							31
32							32
33							33
34							34
35							35

PROBLEM 13-3 ___, Concluded

JOURNAL

PAGE

	DATE		DESCRIPTION	POST. REF.	DEBIT	CREDIT	
1							1
2							2
3							3
4							4
5							5
6							6
7							7
8							8
9							9
10							10
11							11
12							12
13							13
14							14
15							15
16							16
17							17
18							18
19							19
20							20
21							21
22							22
23							23
24							24
25							25
26							26
27							27
28							28
29							29
30							30
31							31
32							32
33							33
34							34
35							35
36							36

PROBLEM 13-4 ___

1. and 2.

Common Stock

Paid-In Capital in Excess of Stated Value—Common Stock

Retained Earnings

Treasury Stock

PROBLEM 13-4 ___, Continued

Paid-In Capital from Sale of Treasury Stock

Stock Dividends Distributable

Stock Dividends

Cash Dividends

PROBLEM 13-4 ___, Continued

2.

JOURNAL PAGE

	DATE		DESCRIPTION	POST. REF.	DEBIT	CREDIT	
1							1
2							2
3							3
4							4
5							5
6							6
7							7
8							8
9							9
10							10
11							11
12							12
13							13
14							14
15							15
16							16
17							17
18							18
19							19
20							20
21							21
22							22
23							23
24							24
25							25
26							26
27							27
28							28
29							29
30							30
31							31
32							32
33							33
34							34
35							35

PROBLEM 13-4 ___, Continued

JOURNAL

PAGE

	DATE		DESCRIPTION	POST. REF.	DEBIT	CREDIT	
1							1
2							2
3							3
4							4
5							5
6							6
7							7
8							8
9							9
10							10
11							11
12							12
13							13
14							14
15							15
16							16
17							17
18							18
19							19
20							20
21							21
22							22
23							23
24							24
25							25
26							26
27							27
28							28
29							29
30							30
31							31
32							32
33							33
34							34
35							35
36							36

PROBLEM 13-4 ___, Concluded

3.

Retained Earnings Statement

4.

This Page Not Used.

PROBLEM 13-5 ___

JOURNAL

PAGE

DATE		DESCRIPTION	POST. REF.	DEBIT	CREDIT

PROBLEM 13-5 ___, Concluded

JOURNAL

PAGE

	DATE		DESCRIPTION	POST. REF.	DEBIT	CREDIT	
1							1
2							2
3							3
4							4
5							5
6							6
7							7
8							8
9							9
10							10
11							11
12							12
13							13
14							14
15							15
16							16
17							17
18							18
19							19
20							20
21							21
22							22
23							23
24							24
25							25
26							26
27							27
28							28
29							29
30							30
31							31
32							32
33							33
34							34
35							35
36							36

EXERCISE 14-1

	a.	b.	c.
Earnings before bond interest and income tax	$	$	$
Less: Bond interest			
Balance	$	$	$
Less: Income tax			
Net income	$	$	$
Less: Dividends on preferred stock			
Earnings available for common stock	$	$	$
Divided by: Shares of common stock outstanding			
Earnings per share on common stock	$	$	$

EXERCISE 14-2

EXERCISE 14-3

EXERCISE 14-4

EXERCISE 14-5

JOURNAL PAGE

	DATE		DESCRIPTION	POST. REF.	DEBIT	CREDIT	
1							1
2							2
3							3
4							4
5							5
6							6
7							7
8							8
9							9
10							10

EXERCISE 14-6

a. 1. through 3.

JOURNAL PAGE

	DATE		DESCRIPTION	POST. REF.	DEBIT	CREDIT	
1							1
2							2
3							3
4							4
5							5
6							6
7							7
8							8
9							9
10							10
11							11
12							12

b.

EXERCISE 14-6, Concluded

c. ______________________

EXERCISE 14-7

a. and b.

JOURNAL PAGE

	DATE		DESCRIPTION	POST. REF.	DEBIT	CREDIT	
1							1
2							2
3							3
4							4
5							5
6							6
7							7
8							8
9							9
10							10

c. ______________________

EXERCISE 14-8

JOURNAL PAGE

	DATE		DESCRIPTION	POST. REF.	DEBIT	CREDIT	
1							1
2							2
3							3
4							4
5							5
6							6
7							7
8							8
9							9
10							10
11							11
12							12
13							13

EXERCISE 14-9

JOURNAL PAGE

	DATE		DESCRIPTION	POST. REF.	DEBIT	CREDIT	
1							1
2							2
3							3
4							4
5							5
6							6
7							7
8							8
9							9
10							10
11							11
12							12
13							13

Name ______________________________

EXERCISE 14-10

a. 1. and 2.

JOURNAL

PAGE

	DATE		DESCRIPTION	POST. REF.	DEBIT	CREDIT	
1							1
2							2
3							3
4							4
5							5
6							6
7							7
8							8
9							9
10							10

b. ______________________________

EXERCISE 14-11

JOURNAL PAGE

	DATE		DESCRIPTION	POST. REF.	DEBIT	CREDIT	
1							1
2							2
3							3
4							4
5							5
6							6
7							7
8							8
9							9
10							10
11							11
12							12
13							13
14							14
15							15

EXERCISE 14-12

a.

Amortization of Installment Notes					
For the Year Ending	A January 1 Carrying Amount	B Note Payment (Cash Paid)	C Interest Expense (7% of January 1 Note Carrying Amount)	D Decrease in Notes Payable (B – C)	E December 31 Carrying Amount (A – D)

EXERCISE 14-12, Concluded

b.

JOURNAL PAGE

DATE		DESCRIPTION	POST. REF.	DEBIT	CREDIT

c. ____

____

EXERCISE 14-13

1. ____________________

2. ____________________

EXERCISE 14-14

a. ____________________

b. ____________________

EXERCISE 14-15

a.

b.

EXERCISE 14-16

a.

b.

APPENDIX 1 EXERCISE 14-17

a. ______________________

____

b. ______________________

____

____

APPENDIX 1 EXERCISE 14-18

a.

b. ______________________

____

c. ______________________

____

____

____

APPENDIX 1 EXERCISE 14-19

____

____

APPENDIX 1 EXERCISE 14-20

____

____

____

____

____

____

____

APPENDIX 1 EXERCISE 14-21

APPENDIX 1 EXERCISE 14-22

APPENDIX 2 EXERCISE 14-23

a. 1. through 3.

JOURNAL PAGE

	DATE		DESCRIPTION	POST. REF.	DEBIT	CREDIT	
1							1
2							2
3							3
4							4
5							5
6							6
7							7
8							8
9							9
10							10
11							11
12							12
13							13
14							14
15							15

b.

c. ____

APPENDIX 2 EXERCISE 14-24

a. 1. through 3.

JOURNAL PAGE

	DATE		DESCRIPTION	POST. REF.	DEBIT	CREDIT	
1							1
2							2
3							3
4							4
5							5
6							6
7							7
8							8
9							9
10							10
11							11
12							12
13							13
14							14
15							15

b.

c. ____

APPENDIX 1 AND 2 EXERCISE 14-25

a. through d.

APPENDIX 1 AND 2 EXERCISE 14-26

a. through d.

This Page Not Used.

PROBLEM 14-1 ___

1.

	Plan 1	Plan 2	Plan 3
Earnings before interest and income tax	$	$	$
Deduct: Interest on bonds			
Income before income tax	$	$	$
Deduct: Income tax			
Net income	$	$	$
Deduct: Dividends on preferred stock			
Available for dividends on common stock	$	$	$
Divided by: Shares of common stock outstanding			
Earnings per share on common stock	$	$	$

2.

	Plan 1	Plan 2	Plan 3
Earnings before interest and income tax	$	$	$
Deduct: Interest on bonds			
Income before income tax	$	$	$
Deduct: Income tax			
Net income	$	$	$
Deduct: Dividends on preferred stock			
Available for dividends on common stock	$	$	$
Divided by: Shares of common stock outstanding			
Earnings per share on common stock	$	$	$

PROBLEM 14-1 ___, Concluded

3. ____________________

PROBLEM 14-2 ___

1. and 2.

JOURNAL PAGE

	DATE		DESCRIPTION	POST. REF.	DEBIT	CREDIT	
1							1
2							2
3							3
4							4
5							5
6							6
7							7
8							8
9							9
10							10
11							11
12							12
13							13
14							14
15							15

3. ______________________________

4. ______________________________

5.

This Page Not Used.

PROBLEM 14-3 ___

1. and 2.

JOURNAL PAGE

	DATE		DESCRIPTION	POST. REF.	DEBIT	CREDIT	
1							1
2							2
3							3
4							4
5							5
6							6
7							7
8							8
9							9
10							10
11							11
12							12
13							13
14							14
15							15

3. ______________________________

4. ______________________________

____

____

____

____

5.

This Page Not Used.

PROBLEM 14-4 ___

1.

JOURNAL

PAGE

	DATE		DESCRIPTION	POST. REF.	DEBIT	CREDIT	
1							1
2							2
3							3
4							4
5							5
6							6
7							7
8							8
9							9
10							10
11							11
12							12
13							13
14							14
15							15
16							16
17							17
18							18
19							19
20							20
21							21
22							22
23							23
24							24
25							25
26							26
27							27
28							28
29							29
30							30
31							31
32							32
33							33
34							34
35							35

PROBLEM 14-4 ___, Continued

JOURNAL

PAGE

DATE		DESCRIPTION	POST. REF.	DEBIT	CREDIT

PROBLEM 14-4 ___, Concluded

2. (a) 2016: ____

(b) 2017: ____

3.

This Page Not Used.

APPENDIX 1 AND 2 PROBLEM 14-5 ___

1. and 2.

JOURNAL

PAGE

	DATE		DESCRIPTION	POST. REF.	DEBIT	CREDIT	
1							1
2							2
3							3
4							4
5							5
6							6
7							7
8							8
9							9
10							10
11							11
12							12
13							13
14							14
15							15
16							16
17							17
18							18
19							19
20							20

3. ____

This Page Not Used.

APPENDIX 1 AND 2 PROBLEM 14-6 ___

1. and 2.

JOURNAL PAGE

DATE		DESCRIPTION	POST. REF.	DEBIT	CREDIT

3. ____

This Page Not Used.

EXERCISE 15-1

a. through d.

JOURNAL PAGE

	DATE		DESCRIPTION	POST. REF.	DEBIT	CREDIT	
1							1
2							2
3							3
4							4
5							5
6							6
7							7
8							8
9							9
10							10
11							11
12							12
13							13
14							14
15							15
16							16
17							17
18							18
19							19
20							20
21							21
22							22
23							23
24							24
25							25

EXERCISE 15-2

a. through d.

JOURNAL

PAGE

	DATE		DESCRIPTION	POST. REF.	DEBIT	CREDIT	
1							1
2							2
3							3
4							4
5							5
6							6
7							7
8							8
9							9
10							10
11							11
12							12
13							13
14							14
15							15
16							16
17							17
18							18
19							19
20							20
21							21
22							22
23							23
24							24
25							25

Name ______________________________

EXERCISE 15-3

a. through d.

JOURNAL

PAGE

DATE	DESCRIPTION	POST. REF.	DEBIT	CREDIT

EXERCISE 15-4

a. and b.

JOURNAL

PAGE

	DATE		DESCRIPTION	POST. REF.	DEBIT	CREDIT	
1							1
2							2
3							3
4							4
5							5
6							6
7							7
8							8
9							9
10							10
11							11
12							12
13							13
14							14
15							15
16							16
17							17
18							18
19							19
20							20
21							21
22							22
23							23
24							24
25							25
26							26
27							27
28							28
29							29
30							30
31							31
32							32
33							33
34							34
35							35

EXERCISE 15-5

EXERCISE 15-6

a., b., and c.

JOURNAL

PAGE

	DATE		DESCRIPTION	POST. REF.	DEBIT	CREDIT	
1							1
2							2
3							3
4							4
5							5
6							6
7							7
8							8
9							9
10							10
11							11
12							12
13							13
14							14
15							15
16							16
17							17
18							18

EXERCISE 15-7

JOURNAL

PAGE

	DATE		DESCRIPTION	POST. REF.	DEBIT	CREDIT	
1							1
2							2
3							3
4							4
5							5
6							6
7							7
8							8
9							9
10							10
11							11
12							12
13							13
14							14
15							15
16							16
17							17
18							18

EXERCISE 15-8

JOURNAL

PAGE

	DATE		DESCRIPTION	POST. REF.	DEBIT	CREDIT	
1							1
2							2
3							3
4							4
5							5
6							6
7							7
8							8
9							9
10							10
11							11
12							12
13							13
14							14
15							15
16							16
17							17
18							18
19							19
20							20
21							21
22							22
23							23
24							24
25							25
26							26
27							27
28							28
29							29
30							30
31							31
32							32
33							33
34							34
35							35
36							36

EXERCISE 15-9

JOURNAL

PAGE

	DATE		DESCRIPTION	POST. REF.	DEBIT	CREDIT	
1							1
2							2
3							3
4							4
5							5
6							6
7							7
8							8
9							9
10							10
11							11
12							12
13							13
14							14
15							15
16							16
17							17
18							18
19							19
20							20
21							21
22							22
23							23
24							24
25							25
26							26
27							27
28							28
29							29
30							30
31							31
32							32
33							33
34							34
35							35
36							36

EXERCISE 15-10

a.

JOURNAL

PAGE

	DATE		DESCRIPTION	POST. REF.	DEBIT	CREDIT	
1							1
2							2
3							3
4							4
5							5
6							6
7							7
8							8
9							9
10							10
11							11
12							12
13							13
14							14

b. ______________________________

EXERCISE 15-11

a.

JOURNAL PAGE

	DATE		DESCRIPTION	POST. REF.	DEBIT	CREDIT	
1							1
2							2
3							3
4							4
5							5
6							6
7							7
8							8
9							9
10							10
11							11
12							12
13							13
14							14
15							15
16							16
17							17
18							18
19							19
20							20

b.

EXERCISE 15-12

a.

JOURNAL PAGE

	DATE		DESCRIPTION	POST. REF.	DEBIT	CREDIT	
1							1
2							2
3							3
4							4
5							5
6							6
7							7
8							8
9							9
10							10
11							11
12							12
13							13
14							14
15							15
16							16
17							17
18							18

b.

EXERCISE 15-12, Concluded

c.

EXERCISE 15-13

EXERCISE 15-14

JED Capital Inc.

Selected Income Statement Items

For the Years Ended December 31, 2016 and 2017

	2016	2017
Operating income	a. __________	e. __________
Unrealized gain (loss)	b. __________	$(11,000)
Net income	c. __________	28,000

JED Capital Inc.

Selected Balance Sheet Items

December 31, 2015, 2016, and 2017

	Dec. 31, 2015	Dec. 31, 2016	Dec. 31, 2017
Trading investments, at cost	$144,000	$168,000	$205,000
Valuation allowance for trading investments	(12,000)	17,000	g. __________
Trading investments, at fair value	d. __________	f. __________	h. __________
Retained earnings	$210,000	$245,000	i. __________

EXERCISE 15-15

a.

JOURNAL PAGE

	DATE		DESCRIPTION	POST. REF.	DEBIT	CREDIT	
1							1
2							2
3							3
4							4
5							5
6							6
7							7
8							8
9							9
10							10
11							11
12							12
13							13
14							14
15							15

b. ____

EXERCISE 15-16

a. and b.

JOURNAL

PAGE

	DATE		DESCRIPTION	POST. REF.	DEBIT	CREDIT	
1							1
2							2
3							3
4							4
5							5
6							6
7							7
8							8
9							9
10							10
11							11
12							12
13							13
14							14
15							15
16							16
17							17
18							18

EXERCISE 15-17

a.

JOURNAL PAGE

	DATE		DESCRIPTION	POST. REF.	DEBIT	CREDIT	
1							1
2							2
3							3
4							4
5							5

Computations:

b. ______________________________

EXERCISE 15-18

a. and b.

EXERCISE 15-19

Highland Industries Inc.

Selected Income Statement Items

For the Years Ended December 31, 2016 and 2017

	2016	2017
Operating income	a. ________	g. ________
Gain (loss) from sale of investments	$7,500	$(12,000)
Net income (loss)	b. ________	(21,000)

Highland Industries Inc.

Selected Balance Sheet Items

December 31, 2015, 2016, and 2017

	Dec. 31, 2015	Dec. 31, 2016	Dec. 31, 2017
Assets			
Available-for-sale investments, at cost	$ 90,000	$ 86,000	$102,000
Valuation allowance for available-for-sale investments	12,000	(11,000)	h. ________
Available-for-sale investments, at fair value	c. ________	e. ________	i. ________
Stockholders' Equity			
Unrealized gain (loss) on available-for-sale investments	d. ________	f. ________	(16,400)
Retained earnings	$175,400	$220,000	j. ________

EXERCISE 15-20

a.

JOURNAL PAGE

	DATE		DESCRIPTION	POST. REF.	DEBIT	CREDIT	
1							1
2							2
3							3
4							4
5							5
6							6
7							7
8							8
9							9
10							10
11							11
12							12
13							13
14							14
15							15

b.

EXERCISE 15-21

a. 1. and 2.

JOURNAL

PAGE

	DATE		DESCRIPTION	POST. REF.	DEBIT	CREDIT	
1							1
2							2
3							3
4							4
5							5
6							6
7							7
8							8
9							9
10							10
11							11
12							12
13							13
14							14
15							15

b. ______________________________

EXERCISE 15-22

a.

JOURNAL PAGE

	DATE		DESCRIPTION	POST. REF.	DEBIT	CREDIT	
1							1
2							2
3							3
4							4
5							5
6							6
7							7

Computations:

b. ______________________________

EXERCISE 15-23

a.

Balance Sheet (selected items)

b.

Balance Sheet (selected items)

EXERCISE 15-24

Balance Sheet (selected Stockholders' Equity items)

EXERCISE 15-25

EXERCISE 15-26

a. Current Year: Dividend Yield: ______________________

Previous Year: Dividend Yield: ______________________

b. ______________________

EXERCISE 15-27

APPENDIX EXERCISE 15-28

APPENDIX EXERCISE 15-29

PROBLEM 15-1 ___

1.

JOURNAL

PAGE

DATE		DESCRIPTION	POST. REF.	DEBIT	CREDIT

PROBLEM 15-1 ___, Continued

JOURNAL

PAGE

	DATE		DESCRIPTION	POST. REF.	DEBIT	CREDIT	
1							1
2							2
3							3
4							4
5							5
6							6
7							7
8							8
9							9
10							10
11							11
12							12
13							13
14							14
15							15
16							16
17							17
18							18
19							19
20							20
21							21
22							22
23							23
24							24
25							25
26							26
27							27
28							28
29							29
30							30
31							31
32							32
33							33
34							34
35							35
36							36

PROBLEM 15-1 ___, Concluded

2. ____

This Page Not Used.

PROBLEM 15-2 ___

1.

JOURNAL

PAGE

	DATE		DESCRIPTION	POST. REF.	DEBIT	CREDIT	
1							1
2							2
3							3
4							4
5							5
6							6
7							7
8							8
9							9
10							10
11							11
12							12
13							13
14							14
15							15
16							16
17							17
18							18
19							19
20							20
21							21
22							22
23							23
24							24

Calculations:

PROBLEM 15-2 ___, Continued

JOURNAL

PAGE

	DATE		DESCRIPTION	POST. REF.	DEBIT	CREDIT	
1							1
2							2
3							3
4							4
5							5
6							6
7							7
8							8
9							9
10							10
11							11
12							12
13							13
14							14
15							15
16							16
17							17
18							18
19							19
20							20
21							21
22							22
23							23
24							24
25							25
26							26
27							27
28							28
29							29
30							30
31							31
32							32
33							33
34							34
35							35
36							36

PROBLEM 15-2 ___, Concluded

2.

Balance Sheet (selected items)

3. ______________________________

This Page Not Used.

PROBLEM 15-3 ___

1.

JOURNAL

PAGE

	DATE		DESCRIPTION	POST. REF.	DEBIT	CREDIT	
1							1
2							2
3							3
4							4
5							5
6							6
7							7
8							8
9							9
10							10
11							11
12							12
13							13
14							14
15							15
16							16
17							17
18							18
19							19
20							20
21							21
22							22
23							23
24							24
25							25
26							26
27							27
28							28
29							29
30							30
31							31
32							32
33							33
34							34
35							35

PROBLEM 15-3 ___, Continued

JOURNAL

PAGE

DATE		DESCRIPTION	POST. REF.	DEBIT	CREDIT

PROBLEM 15-3 ___, Concluded

2.

Balance Sheet (selected items)

This Page Not Used.

PROBLEM 15-4 ___

a. ______________________

b. ______________________

c. ______________________

d. ______________________

e. ______________________

f. ______________________

g. ______________________

h. ______________________

i. ______________________

Calculations:

PROBLEM 15-4 ___, Continued

Completed comparative unclassified balance sheet (optional):

Balance Sheet

	DEC. 31, 2017	DEC. 31, 2016

Name ______________________________

PROBLEM 15-4 ___, Concluded

Calculations:

This Page Not Used.

COMPREHENSIVE PROBLEM 4

1.

JOURNAL

PAGE

	DATE		DESCRIPTION	POST. REF.	DEBIT	CREDIT	
1							1
2							2
3							3
4							4
5							5
6							6
7							7
8							8
9							9
10							10
11							11
12							12
13							13
14							14
15							15
16							16
17							17
18							18
19							19
20							20
21							21
22							22
23							23
24							24
25							25
26							26
27							27
28							28
29							29
30							30
31							31
32							32
33							33
34							34
35							35

COMPREHENSIVE PROBLEM 4, Continued

JOURNAL

PAGE

	DATE		DESCRIPTION	POST. REF.	DEBIT	CREDIT	
1							1
2							2
3							3
4							4
5							5
6							6
7							7
8							8
9							9
10							10
11							11
12							12
13							13
14							14
15							15
16							16
17							17
18							18
19							19
20							20
21							21
22							22
23							23
24							24
25							25
26							26
27							27
28							28
29							29
30							30
31							31
32							32
33							33
34							34
35							35
36							36

COMPREHENSIVE PROBLEM 4, Continued

JOURNAL

PAGE

DATE		DESCRIPTION	POST. REF.	DEBIT	CREDIT

COMPREHENSIVE PROBLEM 4, Continued

JOURNAL

PAGE

	DATE		DESCRIPTION	POST. REF.	DEBIT	CREDIT	
1							1
2							2
3							3
4							4
5							5
6							6
7							7
8							8
9							9
10							10
11							11
12							12
13							13
14							14
15							15
16							16
17							17
18							18
19							19
20							20
21							21
22							22
23							23
24							24
25							25
26							26
27							27
28							28
29							29
30							30
31							31
32							32
33							33
34							34
35							35
36							36

COMPREHENSIVE PROBLEM 4, Continued

2. a.

Income Statement

COMPREHENSIVE PROBLEM 4, Continued

Income Statement (continued)

COMPREHENSIVE PROBLEM 4, Continued

b.

Retained Earnings Statement

COMPREHENSIVE PROBLEM 4, Continued

c.

Balance Sheet

COMPREHENSIVE PROBLEM 4, Continued

Balance Sheet (continued)

COMPREHENSIVE PROBLEM 4, Concluded

Balance Sheet (continued)

EXERCISE 16-1

EXERCISE 16-2

a. ______
b. ______
c. ______
d. ______
e. ______
f. ______
g. ______
h. ______

EXERCISE 16-3

a. Net income: ______
b. Paid cash dividends: ______
c. Issued common stock: ______
d. Issued bonds: ______
e. Redeemed bonds: ______
f. Sold long-term investments: ______
g. Purchased treasury stock: ______
h. Sold equipment: ______
i. Issued preferred stock: ______
j. Purchased buildings: ______
k. Purchased patents: ______

EXERCISE 16-4

a. Decrease in merchandise inventory: ____________________
b. Increase in accounts receivable: ____________________
c. Increase in accounts payable: ____________________
d. Loss on retirement of long-term debt: ____________________
e. Depreciation of fixed assets: ____________________
f. Decrease in notes receivable due in 60 days from customers: ____________________
g. Increase in salaries payable: ____________________
h. Decrease in prepaid expenses: ____________________
i. Amortization of patent: ____________________
j. Increase in notes payable due in 120 days to vendors: ____________________
k. Gain on disposal of fixed assets: ____________________

EXERCISE 16-5

a.

EXERCISE 16-5, Concluded

b. ______________________________

EXERCISE 16-6

a.

b. ______________________________

EXERCISE 16-7

a.

b.

EXERCISE 16-8

EXERCISE 16-9

EXERCISE 16-10

EXERCISE 16-11

EXERCISE 16-12

EXERCISE 16-13

EXERCISE 16-14

EXERCISE 16-15

a.

b.

EXERCISE 16-16

a.

Cash Flows from Operating Activities

b. ____

EXERCISE 16-17

a.

Statement of Cash Flows

EXERCISE 16-17, Concluded

b.

EXERCISE 16-18

EXERCISE 16-18, Continued

(Optional)

Statement of Cash Flows

EXERCISE 16-18, Concluded

Statement of Cash Flows (continued)

EXERCISE 16-19

a.

b.

c. ____________________

EXERCISE 16-20

EXERCISE 16-21

a.

b.

Name ____________________________________

EXERCISE 16-22

a.

Computations:

EXERCISE 16-22, Concluded

b.

EXERCISE 16-23

Computations:

EXERCISE 16-24

a.

b. ______________________

____

____

____

____

____

EXERCISE 16-25

a.

	RECENT FISCAL YEAR END (all numbers in thousands)

EXERCISE 16-25, Concluded

b. ____________________

c. ____________________

EXERCISE 16-26

This Page Not Used.

Name ____________________

PROBLEM 16-1 ___

Statement of Cash Flows

PROBLEM 16-1 ___, Continued

Statement of Cash Flows (continued)

PROBLEM 16-1 ___, Continued

The use of this form is not required unless so indicated by the instructor.

	A	B	C	D	E
1					
2	**Spreadsheet (Work Sheet) for Statement of Cash Flows**				
3					
4		**Balance,**	**Transactions**		**Balance,**
5	**Account Title**	________	**Debit**	**Credit**	________
6					
7					
8					
9					
10					
11					
12					
13					
14					
15					
16					
17					
18					
19					
20					
21					
22					
23					
24					
25					
26					
27					
28					
29					
30					
31					
32					
33					
34					
35					
36					
37					
38					
39					
40					
41					
42					
43					
44					
45					

PROBLEM 16-1 ___, Concluded

	A	B	C	D	E
1					
2	Spreadsheet (Work Sheet) for Statement of Cash Flows (continued)				
3					
4		Balance,	Transactions		Balance,
5	Account Title	________	Debit	Credit	________
6					
7					
8					
9					
10					
11					
12					
13					
14					
15					
16					
17					
18					
19					
20					
21					
22					
23					
24					
25					
26					
27					
28					
29					
30					
31					
32					
33					
34					
35					
36					
37					
38					
39					
40					
41					
42					
43					
44					
45					

PROBLEM 16-2 ___

Statement of Cash Flows

PROBLEM 16-2 ___, Continued

Statement of Cash Flows (continued)

PROBLEM 16-2 ___, Continued

The use of this form is not required unless so indicated by the instructor.

	A	B	C	D	E
1					
2	**Spreadsheet (Work Sheet) for Statement of Cash Flows**				
3					
4		**Balance, ______**	**Transactions**		**Balance, ______**
5	**Account Title**		**Debit**	**Credit**	
6					
7					
8					
9					
10					
11					
12					
13					
14					
15					
16					
17					
18					
19					
20					
21					
22					
23					
24					
25					
26					
27					
28					
29					
30					
31					
32					
33					
34					
35					
36					
37					
38					
39					
40					
41					
42					
43					
44					
45					

PROBLEM 16-2 ___, Concluded

	A	B	C	D	E
1					
2	**Spreadsheet (Work Sheet) for Statement of Cash Flows (continued)**				
3					
4		**Balance,**	**Transactions**		**Balance,**
5	**Account Title**	______________	**Debit**	**Credit**	______________
6					
7					
8					
9					
10					
11					
12					
13					
14					
15					
16					
17					
18					
19					
20					
21					
22					
23					
24					
25					
26					
27					
28					
29					
30					
31					
32					
33					
34					
35					
36					
37					
38					
39					
40					
41					
42					
43					
44					
45					

PROBLEM 16-3 ___

Statement of Cash Flows

PROBLEM 16-3 ___, Continued

Statement of Cash Flows (continued)

PROBLEM 16-3 ___, Continued

The use of this form is not required unless so indicated by the instructor.

	A	B	C	D	E
1					
2	**Spreadsheet (Work Sheet) for Statement of Cash Flows**				
3					
4		**Balance, ______**	**Transactions**		**Balance, ______**
5	**Account Title**		**Debit**	**Credit**	
6					
7					
8					
9					
10					
11					
12					
13					
14					
15					
16					
17					
18					
19					
20					
21					
22					
23					
24					
25					
26					
27					
28					
29					
30					
31					
32					
33					
34					
35					
36					
37					
38					
39					
40					
41					
42					
43					
44					
45					

PROBLEM 16-3 ___, Concluded

	A	B	C	D	E
1					
2	Spreadsheet (Work Sheet) for Statement of Cash Flows (continued)				
3					
4		Balance,	Transactions		Balance,
5	Account Title	____________	Debit	Credit	____________
6					
7					
8					
9					
10					
11					
12					
13					
14					
15					
16					
17					
18					
19					
20					
21					
22					
23					
24					
25					
26					
27					
28					
29					
30					
31					
32					
33					
34					
35					
36					
37					
38					
39					
40					
41					
42					
43					
44					
45					

Name ______________________________

PROBLEM 16-4 ___

Statement of Cash Flows

PROBLEM 16-4 ___, Concluded

Computations:

PROBLEM 16-5 ___

Statement of Cash Flows

PROBLEM 16-5 ___, Concluded

Computations:

EXERCISE 17-1

a.

Comparative Income Statement

	Current Year		Previous Year	
	AMOUNT	PERCENT	AMOUNT	PERCENT

b.

EXERCISE 17-2

a.

Comparative Income Statement (in thousands of dollars)

	CURRENT YEAR		PRIOR YEAR	
	AMOUNT	PERCENT	AMOUNT	PERCENT

EXERCISE 17-2, Concluded

b. ____

EXERCISE 17-3

a.

Common-Sized Income Statement

	TANNENHILL COMPANY		ELECTRONICS INDUSTRY AVERAGE
	AMOUNT	PERCENT	

b.

EXERCISE 17-4

Comparative Balance Sheet

	CURRENT YEAR		PREVIOUS YEAR	
	AMOUNT	PERCENT	AMOUNT	PERCENT

EXERCISE 17-5

a.

Comparative Income Statement

	CURRENT YEAR AMOUNT	PREVIOUS YEAR AMOUNT	INCREASE (DECREASE)	
			AMOUNT	PERCENT

EXERCISE 17-5, Concluded

b. ______________________

EXERCISE 17-6

a. (1) Working Capital = ______________________

Current Year: ______________________

Previous Year: ______________________

(2) Current Ratio = ______________________

Current Year: ______________________

Previous Year: ______________________

(3) Quick Ratio = ______________________

Current Year: ______________________

Previous Year: ______________________

b. ______________________

EXERCISE 17-7

a. (1) Current Ratio = ______________________________

____

Current Year: ______________________________

____

Prior Year: ______________________________

____

(2) Quick Ratio = ______________________________

____

Current Year: ______________________________

____

Prior Year: ______________________________

____

b. ______________________________

____

____

____

____

____

____

____

EXERCISE 17-8

a.

b.

EXERCISE 17-9

a. **(1)** Accounts Receivable Turnover = ______________________________

____

2016: ______________________________

____

2015: ______________________________

____

(2) Number of Days' Sales in Receivables = ______________________________

____

2016: ______________________________

____

2015: ______________________________

____

b. ______________________________

____

____

____

____

____

____

____

____

____

EXERCISE 17-10

a. **(1)** Accounts Receivable Turnover = ______________________________

____

Xavier: ______________________________

____

Lestrade: ______________________________

____

(2) Number of Days' Sales in Receivables = ______________________________

____

Xavier: ______________________________

____

Lestrade: ______________________________

____

EXERCISE 17-10, Concluded

b. ______________________

EXERCISE 17-11

a. **(1)** Inventory Turnover = ______________________

Current Year: ______________________

Preceding Year: ______________________

(2) Number of Days' Sales in Inventory = ______________________

Current Year: ______________________

Preceding Year: ______________________

b. ______________________

Name ______________________________

EXERCISE 17-12

a. (1) Inventory Turnover = ______________________________

____

Dell: ______________________________

____

HP: ______________________________

____

(2) Number of Days' Sales in Inventory = ______________________________

____

Dell: ______________________________

____

HP: ______________________________

____

b. ______________________________

EXERCISE 17-13

a. Ratio of Liabilities to Stockholders' Equity = ______________________________

____

Current Year: ______________________________

____

Previous Year: ______________________________

____

b. Number of Times Bond Interest Charges Are Earned = ______________________________

____

Current Year: ______________________________

____

Previous Year: ______________________________

____

c. ______________________________

____

____

____

____

____

____

EXERCISE 17-14

a. Ratio of Liabilities to Stockholders' Equity = ______________________________

____

Hasbro: ______________________________

____

Mattel, Inc.: ______________________________

____

b. Number of Times Interest Charges Are Earned = ______________________________

____

Hasbro: ______________________________

____

Mattel, Inc.: ______________________________

____

EXERCISE 17-14, Concluded

c. ______________________

EXERCISE 17-15

a. Ratio of Liabilities to Stockholders' Equity = ______________________

Mondelez: ______________________

Hershey: ______________________

b. Ratio of Fixed Assets to Long-Term Liabilities = ______________________

Mondelez: ______________________

Hershey: ______________________

EXERCISE 17-15, Concluded

c. ____________________

EXERCISE 17-16

a. Ratio of Sales to Total Assets = ____________________

YRC Worldwide: ____________________

Union Pacific: ____________________

C.H. Robinson Worldwide Inc.: ____________________

EXERCISE 17-16, Concluded

b.

EXERCISE 17-17

a. Rate Earned on Total Assets = ____________________

2016: ____________________

2015: ____________________

Rate Earned on Stockholders' Equity = ____________________

2016: ____________________

2015: ____________________

Rate Earned on Common Stockholders' Equity = ____________________

2016: ____________________

2015: ____________________

b. ____________________

EXERCISE 17-18

a. Rate Earned on Total Assets = ______________________

Fiscal Year 3: ______________________

Fiscal Year 2: ______________________

b. Rate Earned on Stockholders' Equity = ______________________

Fiscal Year 3: ______________________

Fiscal Year 2: ______________________

c. ______________________

d. ______________________

EXERCISE 17-19

a. Ratio of Fixed Assets to Long-Term Liabilities = ________________________________

b. Ratio of Liabilities to Stockholders' Equity = ________________________________

c. Ratio of Sales to Assets = ________________________________

d. Rate Earned on Total Assets = ________________________________

e. Rate Earned on Stockholders' Equity = ________________________________

f. Rate Earned on Common Stockholders' Equity = ________________________________

EXERCISE 17-20

a. Number of Times Bond Interest Charges Are Earned = ______________________________

b. Number of Times Preferred Dividends Are Earned = ______________________________

c. Earnings per Share on Common Stock = ______________________________

d. Price-Earnings Ratio = ______________________________

e. Dividends per Share of Common Stock = ______________________________

f. Dividend Yield = ______________________________

EXERCISE 17-21

a. Earnings per Share = ____________________

b. Price-Earnings Ratio = ____________________

c. Dividends per Share = ____________________

d. Dividend Yield = ____________________

EXERCISE 17-22

a. Price-Earnings Ratio = ________________________________

Deere & Co.: ________________________________

Google: ________________________________

The Coca-Cola Company: ________________________________

Dividend Yield = ________________________________

Deere & Co.: ________________________________

Google: ________________________________

The Coca-Cola Company: ________________________________

b. ________________________________

APPENDIX EXERCISE 17-23

a. Earnings per share on income before extraordinary items:

Earnings Before Extraordinary Items per Share on Common Stock = ______________________

b. Earnings per Share on Common Stock = ______________________

APPENDIX EXERCISE 17-24

a. ______________________

b. ______________________

c. ______________________

d. ______________________

e. ______________________

f. ______________________

g. ______________________

APPENDIX EXERCISE 17-25

a.

Partial Income Statement

b.

Partial Income Statement

APPENDIX EXERCISE 17-26

a. ______________________________

b. ______________________________

Name ______________________________

PROBLEM 17-1 ___

1.

Comparative Income Statement

	2016	2015	INCREASE (DECREASE) AMOUNT	INCREASE (DECREASE) PERCENT

2. ______________________________

This Page Not Used.

Name ____________________

PROBLEM 17-2 ___

1.

Comparative Income Statement

	2016		2015	
	AMOUNT	PERCENT	AMOUNT	PERCENT

2.

This Page Not Used.

PROBLEM 17-3 ___

1. **a.** Working Capital = ______________________________

   b. Current Ratio = ______________________________

   c. Quick Ratio = ______________________________

PROBLEM 17-3 ___, Concluded

2.

Transaction	Working Capital	Current Ratio	Quick Ratio
a.			
b.			
c.			
d.			
e.			
f.			
g.			
h.			
i.			
j.			

Supporting Data:

Transaction	Current Assets	Quick Assets	Current Liabilities
a.			
b.			
c.			
d.			
e.			
f.			
g.			
h.			
i.			
j.			

PROBLEM 17-4 ___

1. through 19.

1. Working Capital: ______________________________

Ratio	Numerator	Denominator	Calculated Value
2. Current ratio			
3. Quick ratio			
4. Accounts receivable turnover			
5. Number of days' sales in receivables			
6. Inventory turnover			
7. Number of days' sales in inventory			
8. Ratio of fixed assets to long-term liabilities			
9. Ratio of liabilities to stockholders' equity			
10. Number of times interest charges are earned			
11. Number of times preferred dividends are earned			
12. Ratio of sales to assets			
13. Rate earned on total assets			
14. Rate earned on stockholders' equity			
15. Rate earned on common stockholders' equity			
16. Earnings per share on common stock			
17. Price-earnings ratio			
18. Dividends per share of common stock			
19. Dividend yield			

This Page Not Used.

PROBLEM 17-5 ___

1. a.

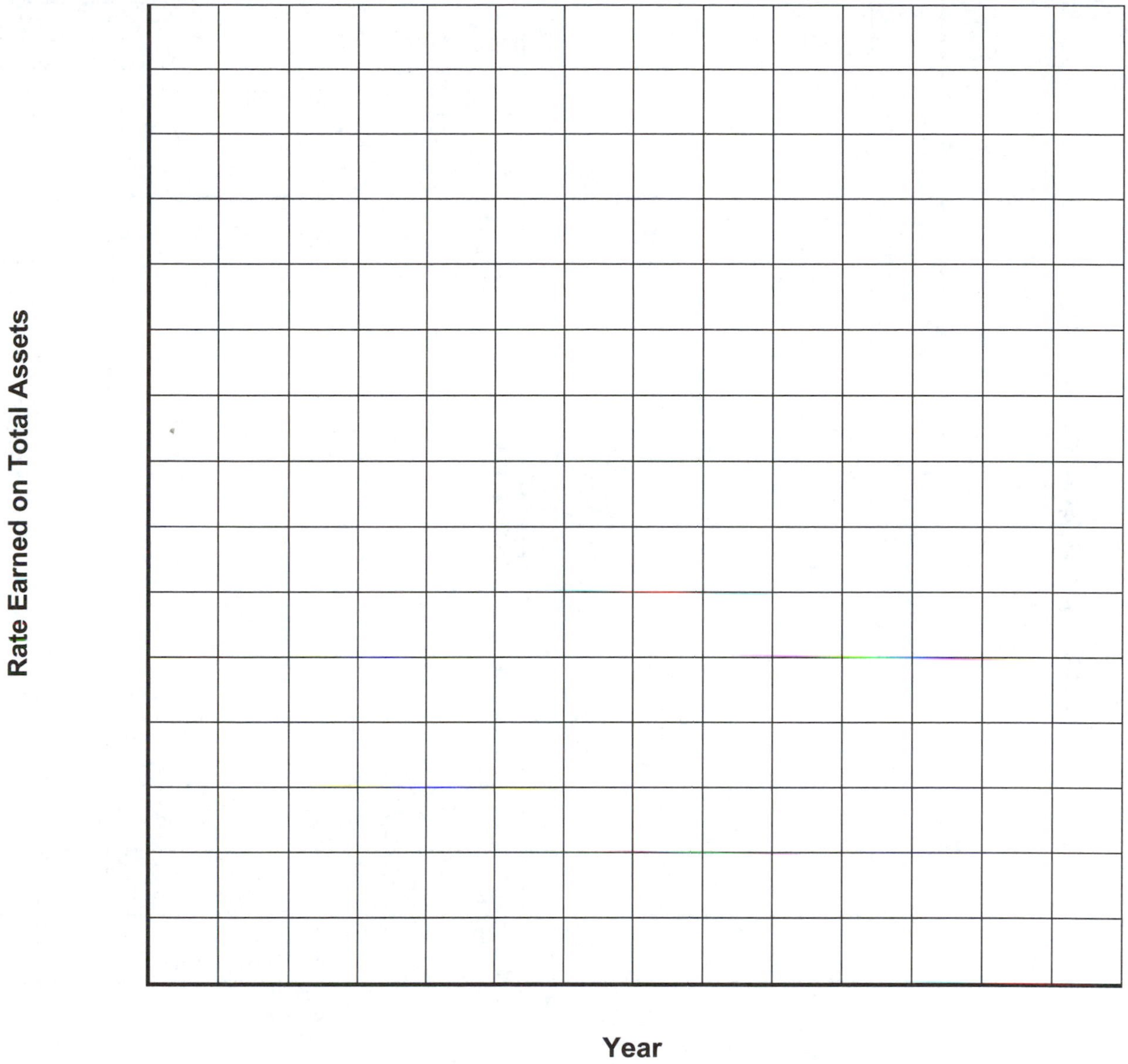

Rate Earned on Total Assets = ____

____

2016: ______________________________

____

2015: ______________________________

____

2014: ______________________________

____

2013: ______________________________

____

2012: ______________________________

____

PROBLEM 17-5 ___, Continued

b.

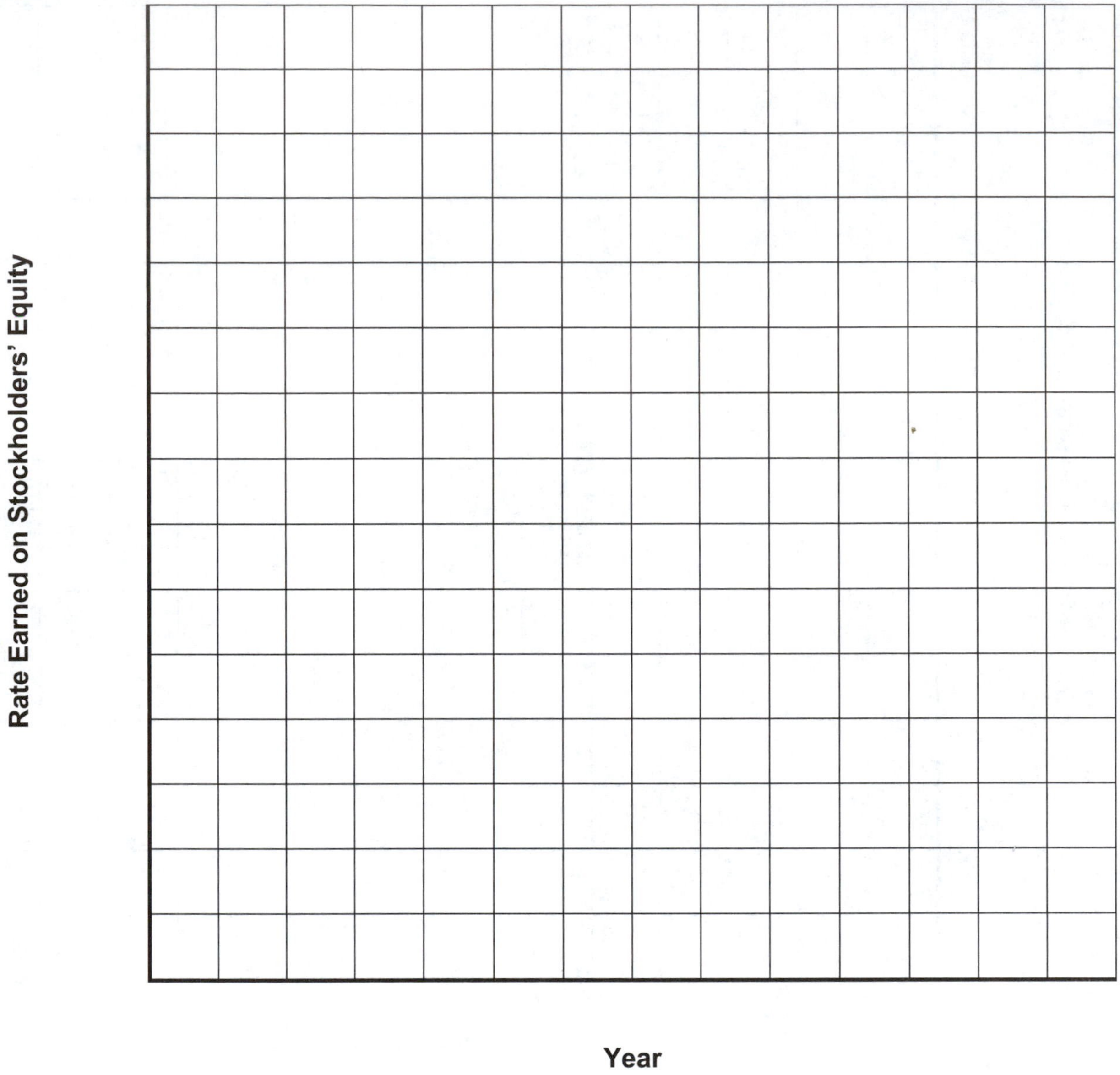

Rate Earned on Stockholders' Equity = ____

____

2016: ______________________________

____

2015: ______________________________

____

2014: ______________________________

____

2013: ______________________________

____

2012: ______________________________

____

PROBLEM 17-5 ___, Continued

c.

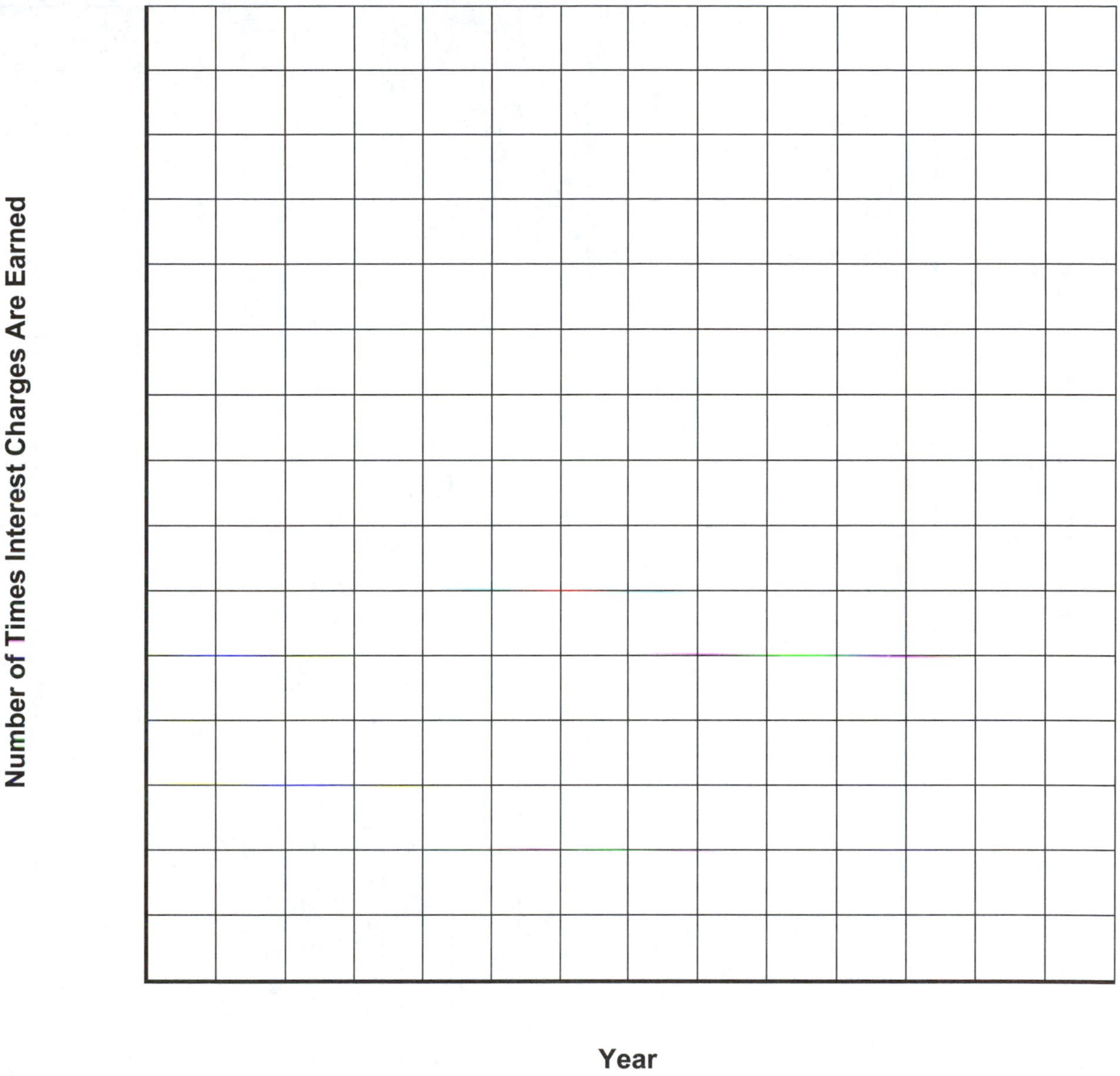

Number of Times Interest Charges Are Earned = ______________________________

____

2016: ______________________________

____

2015: ______________________________

____

2014: ______________________________

____

2013: ______________________________

____

2012: ______________________________

____

PROBLEM 17-5 ___, Continued

d.

Ratio of Liabilities to Stockholders' Equity

Year

Ratio of Liabilities to Stockholders' Equity = ______________________________

____

2016: ______________________________

____

2015: ______________________________

____

2014: ______________________________

____

2013: ______________________________

____

2012: ______________________________

____

PROBLEM 17-5 ___, Concluded

2. ____

This Page Not Used.

NIKE, INC., PROBLEM

1. a. through m.

	FISCAL 2012	FISCAL 2011

NIKE, INC., PROBLEM, Continued

	FISCAL 2012	FISCAL 2011

NIKE, INC., PROBLEM, Continued

	FISCAL 2012	FISCAL 2011

NIKE, INC., PROBLEM, Continued

2. a. through m.

NIKE, INC., PROBLEM, Concluded

This Page Not Used.

Name ______________________________

EXERCISE B-1

a. and b.

JOURNAL PAGE

	DATE		DESCRIPTION	POST. REF.	DEBIT	CREDIT	
1							1
2							2
3							3
4							4
5							5
6							6
7							7
8							8
9							9
10							10
11							11
12							12
13							13
14							14
15							15
16							16
17							17
18							18

EXERCISE B-2

a. and b.

JOURNAL

PAGE

	DATE		DESCRIPTION	POST. REF.	DEBIT	CREDIT	
1							1
2							2
3							3
4							4
5							5
6							6
7							7
8							8
9							9
10							10
11							11
12							12
13							13
14							14
15							15
16							16
17							17
18							18

Name ______________________

EXERCISE B-3

a. (1) ______________________

(2) ______________________

(3) ______________________

(4) ______________________

(5) ______________________

b. (1) through (5)

JOURNAL PAGE

	DATE		DESCRIPTION	POST. REF.	DEBIT	CREDIT	
1							1
2							2
3							3
4							4
5							5
6							6
7							7
8							8
9							9
10							10
11							11
12							12
13							13
14							14
15							15
16							16
17							17
18							18

EXERCISE B-4

a. (1) ______________________

(2) ______________________

(3) ______________________

(4) ______________________

(5) ______________________

b. (1) through (5)

JOURNAL PAGE

	DATE		DESCRIPTION	POST. REF.	DEBIT	CREDIT	
1							1
2							2
3							3
4							4
5							5
6							6
7							7
8							8
9							9
10							10
11							11
12							12
13							13
14							14
15							15
16							16
17							17
18							18